More Than a Holiday

A 25 day Christmas Devotional for the Whole Family

———————

Scott and Sarah Nichols

More Than a Holiday

Copyright © 2013 by Scott Nichols

Edited by Kristin Carter

Cover Art and Book Design by Amanda Cornelius

Corespringdesign.com

Printed in the United States of America

First Printing, 2013

ISBN-13: 978-1492876007

ISBN-10: 1492876003

This book is dedicated to our two sons, Nathan and Asher Nichols.

Table of Contents

Introduction vi

How to Use This Devotional vi

Is the Christmas Story Real?

December 1 How Do I Know Christmas is True.................... 9

December 2 Genealogies 14

December 3 Prophecies 19

The Christmas Story

December 4.. 24

The Characters of the Christmas Story

December 5 Zacharias..34

December 6 Elizabeth.. 39

December 7 John the Baptist...................................... 44

December 8 Herod the Great 49

December 9 Mary - Mother of Jesus 54

December 10 Joseph... 59

December 11 Gabriel 64

December 12 Jesus of Nazareth................................... 68

The Elements of the Christmas Story

December 13 Mary's Magnificat 74

December 14 Zacharias' Prophecy 80

December 15 The Census 85

December 16 No Room at the Inn 90

December 17 The Manger 94

December 18 The Shepherds and Angels 98

December 19 The Magi (Wise Men) 104

December 20 The Magi's Gifts 109

December 21 Simeon and Anna 112

Why is the Christmas Story Important to Us?

December 22 Myths of the Christmas Story 117

December 23 Did Jesus Have a Sin Nature 122

December 24 Why Was This Birth So Important? 127

December 25 Who is Jesus to You? 132

Biography 137

Appendix A 138

Appendix B 142

Appendix C 143

Appendix D 144

References 145

INTRODUCTION

We are excited that you have decided to do this devotional with your family! We pray that it will draw you closer together as a family, open the door for heartfelt discussions, create lasting memories, and help your family grow in their walk with Christ.

This devotional is an intimate look at the nativity story. The first three days answer the question "Is the Christmas Story Real?" The fourth day is a look at the whole story as written in Luke. Days five through twelve examine each character in the Christmas story while days thirteen through twenty-one examine each element of the story. Finally, the last four days answer the question "Why Is the Christmas Story Important to Us?"

Don't rush through it. Take time with your family and work through the devotions and questions. Use the activities to draw younger members of the family into the drama of the birth narrative. Each day is designed to draw your attention to God as you take a more intimate look at the characters and happenings that make up the nativity story.

HOW TO USE THIS DEVOTIONAL

Each devotion is comprised of six different sections. They are designed to be flexible for the needs, constraints, time-limits, and age-range of your family. **You can do one section, or you can do them all.** Families with really young kids may choose to just do the Family Time Activities. Other families may choose to do the whole thing. Make it work for you and what is going to be helpful for your family.

A Closer Look -This section is for the parents. It is meant to be read ahead of time to gain a deeper understanding of the historical context and theological significance behind each topic. It may be helpful for answering questions that come up during the 'Let's Talk' time. If your children are older, they may also benefit from reading this section during their own personal quiet time.

Read - This section tells you what your daily reading will be. It is meant to be read together as a family at the start of the devotion time. Unless otherwise noted, all Scripture used in this book is from the New American Standard Version.

Daily Devotion - The daily devotion is designed to be read aloud as a family. **If you have young kids, you may want to skip the daily devotion altogether** and give a simple summary using pictures from the suggested story books.

Let's Talk –This section is designed with questions to get your family talking. Don't feel constrained by these; they are merely a starting point. Follow the discussion wherever it takes you; it is part of the journey!

Prayer – Next is a simple prayer. It is only a suggestion. Pray together as you feel led to pray. Let your children pray. Sometimes they are the ones with the sweetest, most heartfelt prayers.

Family Time Activities - At the end of every devotion is a list of suggested family time activities. These are designed to bring you together as a family and to create lasting memories. Every day contains a meaningful Christmas song. Spend some time praising God together! If you are musical, break out the instruments.

Most days contain a suggested children's book about the topic. These are great for younger kids. Many of them are available at your local library. You can also go to <u>morethanaholidaydevo.com</u> for information on how to add them to your own collection.

Each day also contains several other activities, including games and crafts, that you could do as a family to drive home the main idea of the lesson. Spend time enjoying being around each other. And don't feel like you have to do all of the activities. They are merely suggestions.

The goal of this project is to provide a resource for families to come together and learn about what Christmas is all about. It is designed to take the focus off of the commercialism and to focus your family on the true meaning of Christmas-the birth of Christ! We pray it blesses you.

DECEMBER 1 How Do I Know Christmas Is True?

 **A CLOSER LOOK**

This is a legitimate question to ask. If you are reading this devotional, then you probably already believe that Christmas is about celebrating the birth of Jesus Christ. But how do we know that Jesus is a real man and that His unbelievable birth story is true?

Since we don't have a living eye-witness from that time period, we must turn to written narrative accounts of Christ's birth from people who were alive at that time. Matthew and Luke were two contemporaries of Jesus who both recorded His birth in the Bible. The Gospel of Matthew records the account with a focus on Joseph, while the Gospel of Luke focuses more on Mary.

Some might argue, however, that the Biblical accounts are just a myth. Fortunately, there are sources of extra-biblical evidence that also record Christ as being a real man. Take one of the most famous Roman historians of the first century, Tacitus, for example. The emperor Nero was persecuting Christians, and Tacitus recorded that these Christians were followers of a man named Christus (Latin for Christ). Tacitus noted that Christus suffered the extreme penalty[1] (a reference to dying on the cross). Tacitus had no reason to make a record of Jesus in his writings; he was writing from a worldview that definitely was pro-Roman, not pro-Christian. The fact that he mentions Christ in his writings is significant.

Another Roman historian, Pliny the Younger, also made record of Christ in his writings.[2] Then there was the Jewish historian, Josephus, who recorded in his annuals a testimony of Jesus in what is called the "Testimonium Flavianun":

> *Now there was about this time Jesus, a wise man, if it be lawful to call him a man, for he was a doer of wonderful works, a teacher of such men as receive the truth with pleasure. He drew over to him both many of the Jews, and many of the Gentiles. He was the Christ; and when Pilate, at the suggestion of the principal men amongst us, had condemned him to the cross, those that loved him at the first did not forsake him, for he appeared to them alive again the third day, as the divine prophets had foretold these and ten thousand other wonderful things concerning him; and the tribe of Christians, so named from him, are not extinct to this day.[3]*

Josephus was a pro-Roman Jew, one that was on the side of Titus during the civil war of A.D. 70. For him to write such things about Christ is quite astounding. Most scholars believe that some of the writing was added by later authors during the Crusades. They believe that enough of the original writing exists, though, to make the case that Christ was a real person who had a large following and was condemned to death by Pontius Pilate (of whom they've found historical evidence proving his existence as a Roman proconsul[4]).

There is overwhelming extra-biblical evidence that Christ was a real person. That evidence lines up with the many things that Scripture says happened at His death. Those parts of Matthew and Luke are corroborated, so we can trust that the birth accounts that are given in the first part of those Gospels are true.

Read	Hebrews 11:1
	Romans 1:16-20

 **DAILY DEVOTION**

It was a brisk December day many years ago that I was just a kid lying on the living room floor thumbing through a book. My father, a tall, thin man, was reading the paper in his chair. "Daddy?" I asked him as he looked up from his paper. "How do we know that Jesus was a real man? What if the stories aren't true?" My father nodded his head, acknowledging my question. He stroked his mustache and gave a small smile before answering. " Sarah," he replied. "We believe that the story is true because we have faith. Hebrews 11:1 says, 'Now faith is the assurance of things hoped for, the conviction of things not seen.'" My father went on, "But faith is nothing if it's not backed in truth. For example, I could make you a big beautiful chair out of toilet paper…" I began to giggle at the thought of my father building a toilet paper chair. "…but no matter how much faith you have that the toilet paper chair will support you when you sit down on it, you will be wrong." My giggles turned into laughter at the thought of falling through a bunch of toilet paper. He continued, "The truth is, toilet paper is flimsy. However, we can have faith that God is real. Just take a look at the intricate detail in everything from the smallest little bug to the massive oceans. In Romans 1:20, it says that you can see that there is a God just by looking at creation."

I still think about that toilet paper chair conversation I had with my father so long ago. He was right. I can believe that Jesus was real because it is recorded in the Bible, which is God's Word. I can trust God because He is the Almighty Creator and His Word is truth.

🚹 LET'S TALK

Do you believe that Jesus was a real man and that His birth story is true?

What do you think Hebrews 11:1 means when it says, "Faith is the assurance of things hoped for"?

How do you know that your faith in Jesus is backed in truth and not a "toilet paper chair" kind of faith?

★ PRAYER ★

Thank you, God, that we can trust Your Word to be true.
Help us to have increasing faith in You.

🏃 FAMILY TIME ACTIVITIES

- Faith Fall - Have one child carefully stand on the edge of a chair or couch with his eyes closed and his arms crossed in front of him across his chest. The rest of the family will stand behind the child with their arms interlocked to catch the child when he falls backwards. Tell the child to stay nice and straight and to fall backwards into your arms. The child must have faith that the rest of the family will catch him.

- Create an obstacle course in your house. It can be simple or complex depending on the age of your children. Blindfold your child and then give him instructions on how to move through the obstacle course. When he reaches the end, talk about how it took faith for the child to listen to the directions and obey them without being able to see. Tell the child that God wants the same kind of faith from us.

- Read *I Wanted to Know All About God* by Virginia L. Kroll.

- Sing "Joy to the World."

DECEMBER 2 — Genealogies

 A CLOSER LOOK

The genealogy passages in the Bible are often considered boring. However, they are critical passages with great vaults of information that can help us to grow in our faith.

Jesus actually has two different genealogies that are recorded. These can be found in Matthew and Luke. There are some differences between the two lists. Most scholars believe that the list found in Matthew 1:1-17 is the lineage of Joseph, which is traced back to Abraham. The list found in Luke 3:23-28 is believed to be the lineage of Mary, which is traced back to the beginning of the world. Matthew's list contains the royal pedigree, while Luke's list contains the blood pedigree.

The Matthew list contains three sets of fourteen different names. The first fourteen deal with the patriarchs of the nation of Israel. The second set of names deals with the establishment of the monarchy, the rise of King David, and the dynasty that he founded. The third set of names deals with the nation conquered by Babylon and the private citizens that helped to run it up until the birth of the Messiah. Jesus' claim to the Davidic throne comes through this royal line. Jesus was not Joseph's biological son, so He was adopted into this line. If it weren't for that adoption, He would have had no claim to the Davidic throne.

David was promised that one of his descendants would sit on his throne and rule for eternity (this is referred to as the Davidic Covenant and is found in 2 Samuel 7:10-13). If Jesus were not of this royal blood line, then that promise would not have been fulfilled. However, the list in Luke shows that Jesus is a descendent of David.

The Luke list is more exhaustive than the Matthew list. This is a regressive list because it starts with Jesus and works its way backwards towards the ancestors. This list goes all the way back to the foundations of history. Through the course of seventy-six generations, Luke traces Christ's pedigree through the kings and patriarchs of Israel, through Noah, through the antediluvian (pre-flood) world, and all the way back to Adam himself.

Why the difference in how the genealogies are recorded? The book of Luke was written to a much wider audience. In fact, the target was the entire Gentile world. Luke wanted to establish that, while Jesus was the Jewish Messiah, He was also here to bring salvation to the rest of the world too, because everyone is descended from Adam.

In ancient Israel, lineage and pedigree were super important. The scholars of the time were well-versed in the Old Testament prophecies regarding the promised Messiah. They knew that the Messiah would come through the tribe of Judah (Genesis 49:10), that He would be from the family line of Jesse (Isaiah 11:1), and that He would be a descendant of the house of David (2 Samuel 7:12). The genealogies of Christ in Matthew and Luke prove that Christ met these prophecies. That is why these lineage passages are so important!

It is also interesting to note that all the documents recording family lines were stored in the Second Jewish Temple. These documents were destroyed in the Jewish rebellion of A.D. 66-70 when the

Roman legions, under Titus, razed the temple. So if anyone came forward claiming to be the Jewish Messiah after that date, he would have a hard time proving his claims because his connection to the line of David could not be verified.

> **Read** Read what Nathan the prophet tells David in 2 Samuel 7:12-13.

 **DAILY DEVOTION**

Every person in the world is unique and different. In fact, you would not be who you are today if you had a different mother or a different father! Everyone who came before you in your family line (like your grandparents and your great grandparents) make up your lineage. Jesus' lineage is very important because there were many prophecies about it. In Genesis 49:10, we see that Jesus will come from the tribe of Judah. In 2 Samuel 7:12-13, we find out that Jesus will be a descendant of King David. This is why the lineage of Jesus' parents is carefully recorded in Matthew and Luke. We need to know whom Jesus' ancestors are so we can see if they fulfill the prophecies.

I think it's pretty incredible that Jesus' lineage meets all the prophecies that were told about Him hundreds of years earlier, don't you? God knew that Jesus was going to be born hundreds and thousands of years before it actually happened. He knew it because He planned and orchestrated every piece of it. What's even more awesome is He knows the same thing about you! When the earth was first created and God breathed air into Adam, He already knew about and planned for YOU. You are not a surprise to God. He knew your name before the beginning of time. He loves you and calls you child. Now if that's not something to get excited about, then I don't know what is!

♟ LET'S TALK

Why is the lineage of Jesus important?

What do you know about your own lineage?

How does it make you feel to know that God had you planned since the beginning of time?

★ PRAYER ★

Lord, we know that we can trust Jesus' birth story to be true because it fulfills all of the prophecies spoken about the coming Messiah. We praise you because you are in control of all things.

🧍 FAMILY TIME ACTIVITIES

- Create a family tree about your lineage. Go back as many generations as you can.

- Look through family photos and talk about fun memories of relatives.

- Read *Just in Case You Ever Wonder* by Max Lucado or *God Gave us You* by Lisa T. Bergren.

- Sing "Come thou Long Expected Jesus."

3 Prophecies

DECEMBER

A CLOSER LOOK

Prophecy can be defined biblically as the telling of truth. In the Bible, God would sometimes speak to people through prophets. Sometimes it would be a word of knowledge about future events, while other times it would be encouragement for their daily lives. The Old Testament is filled with prophecies about future events, including over three hundred prophecies that were made specifically about the coming Messiah.

Reading through the birth narrative in Matthew, the author quietly tells us that Old Testament prophecy has been fulfilled with the birth of Jesus. For example, in the middle of the 8th century B.C., over seven hundred years before the birth of Christ, God spoke through Hosea saying, "out of Egypt I called my Son" (Hosea 11:1b). In Matthew 2:13-15, Joseph has a dream of an angel telling him to take the family down to Egypt to avoid the coming massacre of the innocents ordered by Herod. Joseph and his family stay down in Egypt until Herod's death. After Herod's death, the family travels back to Nazareth. Leaving Egypt for Nazareth was a fulfillment of Hosea's prophecy.

This is only the first of many prophecies about the Messiah that Jesus fulfilled. The prophet Micah predicted that the Messiah would be born in Bethlehem seven hundred years before He was actually born (Micah 5:2). In Matthew 2:1-6, we see this prophecy fulfilled. At the same time, another prophecy was written by the prophet Isaiah that says the Messiah would be born of a virgin (Isaiah 7:14). We can see this prophecy fulfilled in Matthew 1:18-23. How mind blowing is it to see such remarkable details given about the birth of the Messiah centuries in advance?

There are many prophecies that deal with the birth of the Messiah, but there are more that deal with His death. David wrote in Psalm 22:16 that His hands and feet would be pierced. This was a reference to the crucifixion. David probably wrote this Psalm around 1010 B.C. Crucifixion wasn't a form of capital punishment that was used in that century; the Romans wouldn't use crucifixion for another eight hundred years. John records the fulfillment of this prophecy in John 19:34 and 37.

Another prophecy about Jesus' death was fulfilled when Judas betrayed Christ for thirty pieces of silver (Matthew 27:3-10). In Zechariah 11:11-13, Zechariah predicted this would be the price of betrayal some five hundred years before it happened. This, again, is a very specific detail!

There are hundreds of more specific prophecies like these in the Old Testament. To read more, visit http://www.accordingtothescriptures.org/prophecy/353prophecies.html.

Read	Matthew 2:1-6
	Micah 5:2

🏠 DAILY DEVOTION

Yesterday, we learned that the lineage of Jesus was important because it fulfilled the prophecies about His birth. Do you know what a prophecy is? A prophecy in the Bible is a declared truth from God. Here's a fun fact: there are over three hundred prophecies about Jesus in the Old Testament. That's a lot of prophecies!

Have you ever considered the odds of someone actually meeting all the details in all of the prophecies about Jesus? A man named Peter Stoner, in a book called *Science Speaks*, set out to do just that. He did the math, and the numbers he came up with are astronomical. For one person to meet just eight of the prophecies, the chances are one person in one hundred quadrillion people. Stoner claims that many silver dollars would cover the state of Texas two feet deep. Texas is a big place; I mean a BIG place! Imagine trying to find just one silver dollar in a two feet deep pile across the whole state of Texas. This is the probability of one person meeting only eight of the prophecies about Jesus in the Old Testament. If you do the math on one person meeting just forty-eight of the prophecies, the number becomes 1 with 156 zeros after it. We can't even begin to fathom how big that number is. Your chances of winning the lottery while eating a hotdog or getting struck by lightning while riding an elephant are better than meeting the qualifications to be the Messiah.

All this talk of math and probabilities is to prove a point. The only way for someone to meet these prophecies would be if an outside force was guiding and directing him, and that's exactly what God did. From time eternal past, He was guiding the course of human history until exactly at the right moment He broke through and was born in a very humble way. *Only God could have met these prophecies, and that is what He did in the form of Jesus.*

Jesus's birth wasn't an accident; it was planned for and prophesied about hundreds of year before it happened. God knew that we would need a Savior before *we* even knew it. Aren't you glad that the prophets in the Old Testament gave us those prophecies about the coming Messiah? Without them, we may not understand how truly significant and awesome the birth of Jesus was.

 ## LET'S TALK

What is a prophecy?

Why are the prophecies about Jesus' birth important to us?

Do you think anyone else in the whole world could meet all the prophecies that were written about Jesus?

★ PRAYER ★

Lord, thank You for speaking through the prophets hundreds of years in advance to prepare us for Jesus.

🏃 FAMILY TIME ACTIVITIES

- Find a puzzle that has a lot of pieces in your home. Tell your kids to throw all the puzzle pieces in the air at the same time and try to have them all land in the right place. It will create a giant mess. Explain that the probability of Jesus meeting all the prophecies in the Bible is like having that puzzle land completely put together with every piece in the right place.

- Play "Prophecy Memory." Make a copy of the memory cards in Appendix A and cut them out. Lay them face down on a table and take turns flipping over two cards at a time. When you get a card that matches the prophecy with its fulfillment, you get to keep the match. Take turns until all the cards have been collected. Whoever has the most matches, wins.

- Read *A Baby Born in Bethlehem* by Martha Whitmore Hickman.

- Sing "O Little Town of Bethlehem."

DECEMBER 4 — The Story of Jesus' Birth

*This day's devotion is a script of the whole narrative of the birth story. There are no other activities designed for this day. The story is written out using four readers. If you don't have enough people, or your kids are not old enough to read yet, then just read the story from the accompanying verses. You can also use a simple picture book to walk through the story with your younger kids. Try to read it dramatically with a feel for the emotions that the characters are experiencing. You can print a PDF of this script at morethanaholidaydevo.com

THE CHRISTMAS STORY (LUKE 1:5-80 & LUKE 2:1-20)

Act 1 – The Birth of John the Baptist Foretold

Reader 1: In the time of Herod king of Judea there was a priest named Zechariah, who belonged to the priestly division of Abijah; his wife Elizabeth was also a descendant of Aaron. Both of them were righteous in the sight of God, observing all the Lord's commands and decrees blamelessly. But they were childless because Elizabeth was not able to conceive, and they were both very old.

Reader 2: Once when Zechariah's division was on duty and he was serving as priest before God, he was chosen by lot, according to the custom of the priesthood, to go into the temple of the Lord and burn incense.

Reader 3: And when the time for the burning of incense came, all the assembled worshipers were praying outside. Then an angel of the Lord appeared to him, standing at the right side of the altar of incense. When Zechariah saw him, he was startled and was gripped with fear. But the angel said to him:

Reader 4: "Do not be afraid, Zechariah; your prayer has been heard. Your wife Elizabeth will bear you a son, and you are to call him John. He will be a joy and delight to you, and many will rejoice because of his birth, for he will be great in the sight of the Lord. He is never to take wine or other fermented drink, and he will be filled with the Holy Spirit even before he is born. He will bring back many of the people of Israel to the Lord their God. And he will go on before the Lord, in the spirit and power of Elijah, to turn the hearts of the parents to their children and the disobedient to the wisdom of the righteous—

All: to make ready a people prepared for the Lord."

Reader 1: Zechariah asked the angel, "How can I be sure of this? I am an old man and my wife is well along in years." The angel said to him,

Reader 4: "I am Gabriel. I stand in the presence of God, and I have been sent to speak to you and to tell you this good news. And now you will be silent and not able to speak until the day this happens, because you did not believe my words, which will come true at their appointed time."

Reader 2: Meanwhile, the people were waiting for Zechariah and wondering why he stayed so long in the temple. When he came out, he could not speak to them. They realized he had seen a vision in the temple, for he kept making signs to them but remained unable to speak.

Reader 3: When his time of service was completed, he returned home. After this his wife Elizabeth became pregnant and for five months remained in seclusion.

Reader 1: "The Lord has done this for me," she said. "In these days he has shown his favor and taken away my disgrace among the people."

Act 2 –The Birth of Jesus Foretold

Reader 3: In the sixth month of Elizabeth's pregnancy, God sent the angel Gabriel to Nazareth, a town in Galilee, to a virgin pledged to be married to a man named Joseph, a descendant of David. The virgin's name was Mary. The angel went to her and said,

Reader 4: "Greetings, you who are highly favored! The Lord is with you."

Reader 2: Mary was greatly troubled at his words and wondered what kind of greeting this might be. But the angel said to her,

Reader 4: "Do not be afraid, Mary; you have found favor with God. You will conceive and give birth to a son, and you are to call him Jesus. He will be great and will be called the Son of the Most High. The Lord God will give him the throne of his father David, and he will reign over Jacob's descendants forever; his kingdom will never end."

Reader 1: "How will this be," Mary asked the angel, "since I am a virgin?" The angel answered,

Reader 4: "The Holy Spirit will come on you, and the power of the Most High will overshadow you. So the holy one to be born will be called the Son of God. Even Elizabeth your relative is going to have a child in her old age, and she who was said to be unable to conceive is in her sixth month. For no word from God will ever fail."

Reader 1: "I am the Lord's servant," Mary answered. "May your word to me be fulfilled."

All: Then the angel left her.

Act 3-Mary Visits Elizabeth

Reader 3: At that time Mary got ready and hurried to a town in the hill country of Judea, where she entered Zechariah's home and greeted Elizabeth. When Elizabeth heard Mary's greeting, the baby leaped in her womb, and Elizabeth was filled with the Holy Spirit. In a loud voice she exclaimed:

Reader 2: "Blessed are you among women, and blessed is the child you will bear! But why am I so favored, that the mother of my Lord should come to me? As soon as the sound of your greeting reached my ears, the baby in my womb leaped for joy. Blessed is she who has believed that the Lord would fulfill his promises to her!"

Reader 4: And Mary said:

Reader 1: "My soul glorifies the Lord

and my spirit rejoices in God my Savior,

for he has been mindful

of the humble state of his servant.

From now on all generations will call me blessed,

for the Mighty One has done great things for me—

All: Holy is his name.

Reader 1: His mercy extends to those who fear him,

from generation to generation.

He has performed mighty deeds with his arm;

he has scattered those who are proud in their inmost thoughts.

He has brought down rulers from their thrones

but has lifted up the humble.

All: He has filled the hungry with good things but has sent the rich away empty.

Reader 1: He has helped his servant Israel,

remembering to be merciful

to Abraham and his descendants forever,

just as he promised our ancestors."

Reader 4: Mary stayed with Elizabeth for about three months and then returned home.

Act 4 - The Birth of John the Baptist

Reader 3: When it was time for Elizabeth to have her baby, she gave birth to a son. Her neighbors and relatives heard that the Lord had shown her great mercy, and they shared her joy.

On the eighth day they came to circumcise the child, and they were going to name him after his father Zechariah, but his mother spoke up and said,

Reader 2: "No! He is to be called John."

Reader 4: They said to her, "There is no one among your relatives who has that name." Then they made signs to his father, to find out what he would like to name the child. He asked for a writing tablet, and to everyone's astonishment he wrote,

Reader 1: "His name is John."

Reader 2: Immediately his mouth was opened and his tongue set free, and he began to speak, praising God. All the neighbors were filled with awe, and throughout the hill country of Judea people were talking about all these things. Everyone who heard this wondered about it, asking,

All: "What then is this child going to be?" For the Lord's hand was with him.

Reader 1: His father Zechariah was filled with the Holy Spirit and prophesied:

Reader 3: "Praise be to the Lord, the God of Israel,

because he has come to his people and redeemed them.

He has raised up a horn of salvation for us

in the house of his servant David

(as he said through his holy prophets of long ago),

salvation from our enemies

and from the hand of all who hate us—

to show mercy to our ancestors

and to remember his holy covenant,

the oath he swore to our father Abraham:

to rescue us from the hand of our enemies,

and to enable us to serve him without fear

in holiness and righteousness before him all our days.

And you, my child, will be called a prophet of the Most High;

for you will go on before the Lord to prepare the way for him,

to give his people the knowledge of salvation

through the forgiveness of their sins,

because of the tender mercy of our God,

by which the rising sun will come to us from heaven

to shine on those living in darkness

and in the shadow of death,

to guide our feet into the path of peace."

Reader 4: And the child grew and became strong in spirit; and he lived in the wilderness until he appeared publicly to Israel.

Act 5 -The Birth of Jesus

Reader 2: In those days Caesar Augustus issued a decree that a census should be taken of the entire Roman world. (This was the first census that took place while Quirinius was governor of Syria.) And everyone went to their own town to register.

Reader 4: So Joseph also went up from the town of Nazareth in Galilee to Judea, to Bethlehem the town of David, because he belonged to the house and line of David. He went there to register with Mary, who was pledged to be married to him and was expecting a child.

Reader 3: While they were there, the time came for the baby to be born, and she gave birth to her firstborn, a son. She wrapped him in cloths and placed him in a manger, because there was no guest room available for them.

Reader 1: And there were shepherds living out in the fields nearby, keeping watch over their flocks at night. An angel of the Lord appeared to them, and the glory of the Lord shone around them, and they were terrified. But the angel said to them,

Reader 4: "Do not be afraid. I bring you good news that will cause great joy for all the people. Today in the town of David a Savior has been born to you; he is the Messiah, the Lord. This will be a sign to you: You will find a baby wrapped in cloths and lying in a manger."

Reader 2: Suddenly a great company of the heavenly host appeared with the angel, praising God and saying,

All: "Glory to God in the highest heaven,

and on earth peace to those on whom his favor rests."

Reader 3: When the angels had left them and gone into heaven, the shepherds said to one another,

Reader 1: "Let's go to Bethlehem and see this thing that has happened, which the Lord has told us about."

Reader 4: So they hurried off and found Mary and Joseph, and the baby, who was lying in the manger. When they had seen him, they spread the word concerning what had been told them about this child, and all who heard it were amazed at what the shepherds said to them.

Reader 2: But Mary treasured up all these things and pondered them in her heart. The shepherds returned, glorifying and praising God for all the things they had heard and seen, which were just as they had been told.

★ PRAYER ★

Lord, thank You for the incredible details you placed in Jesus' birth story. Thank you that we can read about it in the Bible. Help us to always understand and remember the real reason we celebrate Christmas.

5 Zacharias

DECEMBER

 **A CLOSER LOOK**

Luke begins his Gospel with the story of the birth of Christ's second cousin, John the Baptist. John's parents were Zacharias and Elizabeth. Zacharias was a priest. There were probably around 20,000 priests serving in Jerusalem around the time of Christ's birth.[5] Many of them, even while working in the temple and being around the things of God, had grown callous in their hearts towards God. Later in His ministry, Jesus called some of them a brood of vipers and white-washed tombs. The priest's leaders (Sadducees and Pharisees) were the ones that had the illegal trials of Christ and handed Him over to Pilate, demanding He be put to death.

Zacharias was different from these priests. He was called righteous before God by Luke. He did everything he could to obey the commands of Scripture and the requirements that God had given in the Law (Luke 1:6). As much as he tried to follow God's commands, Zacharias and his wife had a problem. They had no children. They had no one to carry on their family line. Worst of all, they were old and past the age of having kids (Luke 1:18). At that time, Jewish society looked down on people that did not have any kids. They were thought to be under a curse by God for some sin they had committed. Talk about a burden to carry! Here they are trying to walk blameless before God, and everyone around them is judging them.

According to custom, Zacharias could have divorced Elizabeth and remarried a younger woman to try and get an heir. Instead, he remained faithful to his wife and made his request for a child known to God (Luke 1:13). When he didn't get an answer, he continued to faithfully serve the Lord.

Zacharias was of the priestly division of Abijah (Luke 1:5). The priests had been divided into twenty-four different courses by King David. His division was number eight on the list. Each division would come serve in the temple two times a year in one week intervals. However, with nearly one thousand priests in each division, the chance to serve in the temple probably only came along to each priest once or twice in their lifetimes.[6] When Zacharias's term finally came up, I'm sure he was excited to go serve. While there, he was chosen to enter the Holy Place and offer incense (Luke 1:9). As the incense burned, others would be outside the Holy Place offering up prayers of worship (Luke 1:10). The smoke rising up from the incense symbolized the prayers of the people going up to God in Heaven.

While he was in the Holy Place, the angel Gabriel appeared to him (Luke 1:19). Zacharias was startled, and the angel told him to not be afraid for he had a message filled with great joy. Gabriel announced that Zacharias and his wife were about to have a son, and he would be the one to prepare the way for the Messiah! He was told to name the baby John (Luke 1:11-17).

Zacharias didn't believe Gabriel. Although righteous, he was still a man and prone to doubts in his faith just like the rest of us. Gabriel gave him a sign to validate his message by taking away his ability to speak until John's birth (Luke 1:18-20). As his service in the temple came to an end, he went back home to his wife where he spent the next nine months in silence.   Finally the time came for John to be born. As was custom at that time, he was circumcised on the eighth day and given his name (Luke 1:59). The priests performing the ceremony wanted to name the child after his father, but Elizabeth objected, saying that he was to be named John. The priests questioned her because they had no relatives who were named John (Luke 1:60-61). They went to Zacharias to confirm the name choice, and as he was starting to write the name down, his speech was restored! Two miracles happened in the presence of the people. Elizabeth, an old lady, had given birth to a son, and Zacharias had his speech restored (Luke 1:65). The first words that Zacharias uttered were of praise to God (Luke 1:68-79).

The meaning of Zacharias' name is very interesting. It means "the Lord remembers." God remembered the request of Zacharias and did more than just answer it. He wanted a child to carry on the family name, and instead they had a child who would be the forerunner of the Messiah.

It is interesting that John's name means "the Lord is gracious." God was truly gracious in answering the request of Zacharias. God is gracious in answering our impossible prayer requests too. He is the God of the Impossible!

> # Read   Luke 1:5-24, 57-66

⌂ DAILY DEVOTION

What does the word *impossible* mean? What is something that is impossible for you to do? Today we are going to learn about a man named Zacharias, who was told by God that something impossible would happen.

Zacharias was an old man who loved God very much. He was a priest, and one day he was given the very special job of going into the Holy Place of the temple. In the Holy Place, priests would often offer sacrifices, pray, and worship God. When Zacharias was in the Holy Place, an angel named Gabriel appeared to him out of nowhere and announced to him that he would have a son and that he should name the baby John.

Imagine Zacharias' surprise. He and his wife were too old to have children, yet an angel was telling him that they would have a son! Zacharias could not believe this to be possible, so the angel took away Zacharias' voice as a sign. When he came out of the temple unable to speak, everyone knew that something special had happened.

Nine months later, a bouncing baby boy was born to Zacharias and his wife Elizabeth; it was a miracle! Then, just as the baby was being named, Zacharias' voice came back to him. Another miracle! The first words to come out of Zacharias' mouth were words of praise to God.

I'm sure if Zacharias were still alive today, he would tell you that nothing is impossible with God. His baby would grow up to be known as John the Baptist and would play an important role in preparing the world for Jesus.

ᵀ LET'S TALK

How do you think Zacharias felt when the angel appeared to him in the temple?

Why did God take away Zacharias' voice?

What is something impossible that only God can do?

What should you do when something in your life seems impossible?

★ PRAYER ★

Lord, we thank You that nothing is impossible with You! We praise You for always listening to our requests and providing for our every need.

ᵀ FAMILY TIME ACTIVITIES

- Play charades as a family. Try to get a feel for how Zacharias felt when he was unable to speak.

- Get two members of your family to act out the scene between Zacharias and the angel in the temple.

- Read the page on Zacharias from *Voices of Christmas* by Nikki Grimes.

- Sing "Hark! The Herald Angels Sing."

6 Elizabeth

DECEMBER

 **A CLOSER LOOK**

Yesterday, we looked at Zacharias' response to finding out he would have a son. Today, we will be looking at Elizabeth's response. Elizabeth is first mentioned in Luke 1:5-7. In this section are many biographical details about Elizabeth: She is married to Zacharias. She is called the daughter of Aaron. (This means her father was a priest just like her husband Zacharias.) She is called righteous in the sight of God. She grew up in a household that taught the concept of following the Law as a way to bring praise and honor to God. She is called blameless and made it her mission to follow the commands of God.

She and her husband were very old. She was past her child-bearing years, and they did not have any children. At that time, society looked down on barren women. It was assumed that barren women were being punished by God for sinning.[7] There was probably a lot of shame that she carried around. Yet instead of getting mad at God for the shame and ostracization that she probably suffered, she continued to follow Him and obey his commandments. This speaks greatly to the kind of character she possessed.

Then one day the angel Gabriel appeared to her husband and told him that she would become pregnant and give birth to a son named John. Their son would be the person to prepare the way for the Messiah (Luke 1:13-17). Undoubtedly, Elizabeth was overjoyed by this news.

In Luke 1:26, Mary, the mother of Jesus, is introduced. She was the cousin of Elizabeth. The angel Gabriel told her that she would become pregnant even though she was still a virgin. Mary wondered how this could be, so Gabriel mentioned that Elizabeth had also miraculously become pregnant. Elizabeth's story was used to help strengthen the faith of her cousin Mary.

In Luke 1:39-45, Mary visits Elizabeth. When Elizabeth saw Mary, the Holy Spirit moved John inside of her, and she proclaimed that Mary was to be blessed among women because she carried the Lord in her (Luke 1:42). This statement makes it clear that she understood who Mary's child was. This knowledge was a revelation from the Holy Spirit.

Elizabeth asked humbly why she was so favored that the mother of her Lord should come to visit. (In the passage, she says "my Lord," which is a Messianic reference found in Psalm 110:1.) She understood her place before God, and to be in His presence, even while He was in utero, was a great blessing for her!

Elizabeth is an example of a person with great character. She walked humbly before God and waited faithfully on His timing, even when it brought judgment on her from the rest of society.

Read	Luke 1:24-45

DAILY DEVOTION

When I was a kid, I wanted a pair of roller skates so badly. It seemed like all my friends had roller skates and would go skating around the neighborhood while I was stuck walking or riding my bike. I longed to experience the wind in my braids as I zipped around at super-lightning speeds. I begged my parents with every tactic I could think of. I promised to do more chores; I complained about being the ONLY one without roller skates; I touted the health benefits of the extra exercise I would get with roller skates; I even prayed and asked God for roller skates, but nothing worked. My parents kept telling me that they couldn't afford roller skates right now and that I had to be patient. I was certain I was never going to get them. Then something funny happened. Roller skates started to lose their popularity to the more streamlined roller blades.

That year on my birthday, I opened a finely wrapped package to find a new pair of pink and purple rollerblades, complete with sparkly wheels and a shiny white boot that laced all the way up my ankles. They were AWESOME, and I wore them proudly around the neighborhood as I practiced all my cool skating moves that were a lot harder for my friends to do on their roller skates. The funny thing is, if my parents had given me the roller skates I had asked for at the time that I really wanted them, then they wouldn't have been able to afford the more awesome rollerblades for me a couple of months later. Their timing was so much better than my timing.

Sometimes it's hard to understand why God doesn't answer our prayers right away. I'm sure this is how Elizabeth in the New

Testament felt. She and her husband Zacharias wanted a baby. They prayed and asked God for a baby for many years, but they never had one. People looked down on them and thought God was punishing them by not giving them a baby. Finally, once they were too old to have a baby, God performed a miracle; and Elizabeth became pregnant. Baby John was born at just the right time in history to perform the very special job that God had for him. If he had been born earlier, as Elizabeth and Zacharias had prayed for, he wouldn't have been able to be the world-changer that he was.

Isaiah 55:9 says, "For as the heavens are higher than the earth, so are my ways higher than your ways and my thoughts than your thoughts." God is saying that His ways are better for us than our ways. I'm sure Elizabeth felt this way when she held her newborn baby for the first time.

I no longer have those special roller blades; I grew out of them many years ago. However, the lesson I learned from them will never be forgotten. God's timing is *always* better than our timing!

LET'S TALK

How do you think Elizabeth and Zacharias felt about not having any kids?

How was God's timing for Elizabeth's pregnancy better than her own timing?

Read Isaiah 55:9 again. What do you think it means?

Can you think of a time in your life when God's timing was better than your timing?

★ PRAYER ★

Lord, Your timing is always perfect, even when it doesn't match ours.
Help us to be patient and wait on You.

🚶 FAMILY TIME ACTIVITIES

- Make a list as a family about other Bible characters who had to wait for God's timing in their life.

- Play the Breakfast Scramble Minute-to-win-it Game (http://www.nbc.com/minute-to-win-it/how-to/episode-232/breakfast-scramble/). Tell your kids that since today's lesson was about God's timing, you are going to play a game that is all about timing. There are lots of other Minute-to-win-it games you could play at the Minute-to-win-it website.

- Read the page on Elizabeth from *Voices of Christmas* by Nikki Grimes.

- Sing "O Come O Come Emmanuel."

7 John the Baptist

DECEMBER

A CLOSER LOOK

The first mention of John can be found in Luke 1:13 when Gabriel announces to Zacharias that he will have a son and should name him John. In verses 15-17, Luke describes what John will be like as a man. Verse 15 tells us that he will be great in the sight of the Lord. (In Luke 7:28, Jesus even went so far as to say that no man ever born will be greater than John.) We also find out in that verse that he is going to be a Nazarite from birth, which means that his whole life would be dedicated to the service of God and would be marked by not drinking fermented beverages or cutting his hair. (Sampson and Elijah are the only two other Nazarites from birth mentioned in the Bible.) In verses 16 and 17, Gabriel explains that John will be like Elijah in power and spirit, calling the nation back from its sin and returning to the ways of the Lord. At the end of the chapter, John is born.

The next mention of John is thirty years later when he starts his ministry. Prior to his prophetic ministry, there had not been an active prophet in Israel since the book of Malachi was written over four hundred years earlier. (This is called the four hundred silent years.) John breaks this silence. Matthew quotes from Isaiah 40:3 when he says that John is the voice from the wilderness who would prepare the way for the Lord (Matthew 3:3).

John was a precursor to the Messiah coming by going out and proclaiming the need for people to return to God. He would baptize people in water (where he got his nickname "The Baptist") to symbolize their turning their backs on sins and returning to God (Matthew 3:11). In Matthew 3, Jesus appears and asks John to baptize Him. John immediately recognizes Christ and insists that it is he that should be baptized by Christ instead of the other way around. John eventually consents, though, and baptizes Christ (Matthew 3:13-17).

After this episode, John continues proclaiming the need for people to repent from their sins and return to God. He doesn't stop. Eventually Herod (not the Herod who was king when John was born, but his son, Herod Antipas) has John arrested (this episode is found in Mark 6:18-29). Herod had married his brother's wife in violation of Scripture. John called out the wrongness of the marriage, which caused Herodias, Herod's wife, to want him put to death. While John was in prison, Herodias had her daughter, Salome, dance before the king. Herod loved it so much that he promised the girl anything, including up to half of his kingdom. With consultation from her mother, Salome asked for John's head on a platter. Herod gave in because he didn't want to lose face before his party guests and he wanted to keep his wife happy. Josephus also records this incident in his *Antiquities*.[8] Based on Josephus writings, archeologists have even found the palace where Herod's party happened and where John was beheaded.[9]

John knew what his mission in life was, and he pursued it with boldness and passion. He proclaimed the coming of the Messiah with reckless abandon. He boldly declared his faith, which raises the question – Are we that bold in declaring our faith?

| Read | Luke 1:13-17, 57-66, 80 |
| | Matthew 3:4-6 |

DAILY DEVOTION

Recently an eighteen year old girl named Stormy was told she was not allowed to ride on the school bus anymore. Why? She was the only person to stick up for a middle school student with disabilities who was being bullied on the bus. Stormy reported the bullying to the bus driver and to the school, but the bullying didn't stop. Finally, she told the bullies to leave the girl alone or she would take things into her own hands. This got Stormy removed from the bus. She was doing the right thing and got in trouble for it.[10]

Over fifty years ago, a lady named Rosa Parks was arrested because she refused to give up her seat on the bus. Back then, people were treated differently if their skin was a different color, and Rosa knew this was wrong. By refusing to move, she was standing up for what is right. The bus driver ended up calling the police. Rosa was arrested, but she is now famous for doing the right thing and helping others to be brave enough to do the right thing too.

There have been lots of brave people in history who were punished for doing the right thing. Remember Baby John, Zacharias' and Elizabeth's miracle baby boy? He eventually grew up to become John the Baptist. John the Baptist was Jesus' cousin, and he loved God very much. He spent his whole life telling people about God and baptized a lot of people in the Jordan River, including Jesus. John the Baptist always stood up for what was right, even if no one else would. He was bold and courageous in telling other people about God. He helped prepare many people for Jesus' ministry. One day he told the king and queen that they needed to stop sinning. They did not like to hear him speaking the truth, and so they had him killed for it. What a price to pay for doing what is right!

John the Baptist isn't usually considered one of the important characters in the Christmas story; however, without him, many people may not have been ready to accept Jesus for who He was- God! It was a good thing he was bold enough to stand strong and tell people the truth.

⫟ LET'S TALK

Have you ever stood up for what is right, even when no one else was?

What character qualities would you use to describe John the Baptist?

Why is John the Baptist an important part of the Christmas story?

What is one way you can stand up for what is right this Christmas season?

★ PRAYER ★

*Lord, following Your commands is not easy for us sometimes.
Help us to be strong and to always do what is right.*

🎎 FAMILY TIME ACTIVITIES

- Make a list of all the people you can think of (in history or in your personal life) who did the right thing even if it could have gotten them in trouble.

- Toast some bread, and put some honey and raisins on the top. Eat it together and talk about how John the Baptist was known to live in the wilderness and eat honey and locusts. Pretend that the raisins are locusts.

- Read *His Name is John* by Arch Books or *John the Baptist Prepares the Way for the Lord* by Joy Melissa Jensen.

- Sing "Silent Night."

8 Herod the Great

 A CLOSER LOOK

Herod the Great was the vassal king of Judah under the Romans when Christ was born. He was known for a being a paranoid king who had one of his own wives and sons murdered because he was afraid that they were plotting against him. He was good at playing the Romans and keeping in power because he stayed in their favor. He was known for being an especially brutal king who would not hesitate to have someone killed. He had a grand vision to make Jerusalem a world class city and embarked on a massive building program that was funded by the taxes he levied on his subjects. He was responsible for rebuilding the second temple constructed under Nehemiah. He also was responsible for the construction of the port at Caesarea and various palaces and military fortifications (such as Masada).[11]

Herod was born in 73 B.C. in southern Palestine. He was ethnically an Idumean (earlier in the Bible they were called the Edomites or the descendants of Esau), but religiously he was a Jew. A century prior to his birth, the Hasmonean dynasty had conquered that area of land and had made everyone convert to Judaism or be deported. His father, Antipater, became a client to Pompey. Because of his support, Pompey rewarded the family and put them into a position of power in Judah, allowing them to rule it.[12] During this time, Herod befriended

Mark Antony (of the famed Mark Antony and Cleopatra). A civil war broke out, and he was forced to flee to Rome. While in Rome, the Senate appointed him "king of the Jews." The Senate gave him the forces to return and conquer the province. He conquered Jerusalem in 37 B.C. and ruled it until his death in 4 B.C. During the Roman civil war between Antony and Octavian (the great nephew of Julius Caesar), Herod switched allegiances to Octavian (the future Caesar Augustus). For this, Octavian let him stay in power and remain the vassal king of Judah.

Herod had at least eight wives and fourteen children. His favorite wife was Mariamne, a Hasmonean princess.[13] He had married her to try and legitimize his claim to the throne. She was one of the last daughters of the dynasty that ruled before him. He had two sons by her and intended to make them his heirs. However, through court intrigue by his sister, Salome, he grew distrustful of them and eventually had them murdered. His paranoia and mental instability continued until the day he died.

This was the political leadership of the world that Jesus was born into. After Jesus was born (most likely between 6-4 B.C.), the Magi from the East appeared, guided by the Star (Matthew 2:1). They ask Herod for information about the newborn king of the Jews (Matthew 2:2). This angered Herod since he was the current king of the Jews. It also fueled his paranoia. He told the Magi to go and find the whereabouts of the child and then tell him because he wanted to come and worship the child too (Matthew 2:7-8). After the Magi found baby Jesus and presented their gifts in worship, they had a dream that they should not go back to Herod, but should take a different route home (Matthew 2:12). Joseph also had a similar dream, and he took his family down to Egypt to avoid the coming wrath of Herod (Matthew 2:13-15).

After learning that the Magi had left and not reported to him, Herod was furious! He did not want someone else taking his throne. He gave orders that all boys under the age of two be put to death (Matthew 2:16-18). Jesus was spared because his family had already left for Egypt at the time of the decree. This event is called the Massacre of the Innocents. No other historians record this event. Scholars estimate that only around twenty children died in this incident,[14] and because the numbers were small, they did not record it.

The summation of his life is wrapped up in two words: "Herod died" (Matthew 2:19). Josephus mentioned much more detail about his death, stating that Herod died during a lunar eclipse and was in excruciating pain when he died.[15]

Read   Matthew 2:1-20

DAILY DEVOTION

King Herod was a very jealous and selfish man. He was always worried that someone would try to take over his job as king. He even had his very own wife and children murdered because he suspected that they were plotting against him. One day, some wise men showed up at his palace and asked him if he knew any information about the newborn king of the Jews. Herod was surprised to hear people talking about another king of the Jews, especially since **he** was king of the Jews.

He kindly told the wise men that he didn't know about this new king, but he would love to worship the baby too. (This was a lie.) He asked the wise men to tell him where the new king was once they found him. Inside, Herod became furious with jealousy. How could there be another king of the Jews?! He waited and waited to hear back from the wise men.

After a while, King Herod discovered that the wise men had left without telling him about the baby. In his anger, he decided to have all baby boys from zero to two years old killed, hoping that one of those babies would be baby Jesus. This was called the Massacre of the Innocents. Can you imagine having so much anger and jealousy in your heart that you could kill innocent babies? King Herod must have been a really unhappy, miserable man.

Baby Jesus wasn't killed in the Massacre of the Innocents. An angel appeared to His parents, Mary and Joseph, and told them to leave Bethlehem. God protected Jesus.

⭑ LET'S TALK

What kind of character qualities did King Herod display?

Have you ever been jealous before? When?

Why did King Herod have all the baby boys killed?

How did God protect baby Jesus?

How does God protect you?

★ PRAYER ★

Lord, help us not to be angry or jealous towards others.
Give us grace to love others the way You love them.

FAMILY TIME ACTIVITIES

- Talk about a time being jealous or angry impaired your judgment to make a good decision.

- Take a closed can of soda and pass it around to every member of the family. Have every member of the family shake it while telling a story about a time he was angry or jealous. Then go outside and carefully open the can of soda. Watch it explode all over and create a huge mess. Talk about how, when we let anger and jealousy fester in our hearts without forgiveness, it will eventually come out and affect everyone around you, causing a big, ugly mess.

- Read the page on Herod in the book *Voices of Christmas* by Nikki Grimes.

- Sing "The First Noel."

DECEMBER 9 Mary Mother of Jesus

 **A CLOSER LOOK**

After Jesus, Mary is the most well-known and most written about character of the New Testament. Different religions believe different things about Mary. Some beliefs about Mary are far-fetched, such as the one that says she remained a virgin[16] for the rest of her life (which is impossible since she had other sons and daughters according to Matthew 13:55-56 and Mark 6:3). Other traditional doctrines make statements such as the following: she was free of original sin; she was taken into Heaven like Enoch and Elijah; and she is now entitled to be called Queen because of her relationship to Christ as His mother.[17] In order to really understand Mary, we need to turn to Scripture and use that as our guide.

The first time we see Mary mentioned is in Luke 1:26-38. In this passage, the angel Gabriel appears to Mary. Gabriel delivers the message that Mary will become pregnant and give birth to the Son of God who will sit on David's throne and reign forever (a reference to the Davidic covenant found in 2 Samuel 7:12-13[18]). Mary is shocked! How is she going to have a child, when she is still a virgin? Gabriel responds that the Holy Spirit will make this happen; it will be a miracle from God. This is also in fulfillment of a prophecy that the Messiah would be born of a virgin (Isaiah 7:14). Gabriel then uses Elizabeth's pregnancy as a way to build up Mary's faith. Mary doesn't question Gabriel; instead, she believes right away and declares that she is the Lord's servant and is okay with Gabriel's revelation being fulfilled in her. We do not know how old Mary was when Gabriel appeared to her. We do have some clues from cultural tradition, which states that once young preteens had their Bat-mitzvah, they would be considered women and married off to start having children. It is likely she was between the ages of thirteen and sixteen[19] when she had Jesus.

After Jesus was born, Mary and Joseph traveled to Egypt and then back to Nazareth where they raised Jesus. The only time we see Mary mentioned during His childhood was when Jesus was left at the temple at the age of twelve (Luke 2:41-52). It was during this time that she and Joseph had four more sons.[20]

Eighteen years later, Mary was present at Jesus' first miracle where He turned water into wine (John 2:1). A year and half later, she turned up in Capernaum, where people asked who Christ's brothers and mother were and He turned and pointed at them (Matthew 12:46-50). After that she is not mentioned until she is at the foot of the cross (John 19:26). Jesus is hanging on the cross paying for the sins of the world with His crucifixion. He knows that He will soon die, and He makes arrangements for John to take care of His mother once He has died.

The last time Mary is mentioned in the Bible is after Jesus ascended to Heaven in Acts 1. The disciples, along with Mary and a few other women, return to Jerusalem (Acts 1:14).

Mary was a person of great faith. She never questioned who her child was and trusted God's plan for her life.

Read   Luke 1:26-38

 **DAILY DEVOTION**

Mary, the mother of Jesus, was an incredible woman. An angel appeared to her at a young age and announced that she was going to have a baby. She accepted this news even though she knew that many people wouldn't believe her. There was also the chance that they would judge her for being pregnant before her betrothal to Joseph was over. After all, would you believe someone if she told you she was pregnant with God?

During her pregnancy, Mary went to visit Elizabeth. Remember Elizabeth? She was pregnant with John the Baptist even though she was too old to have a baby. Mary went to Elizabeth because, if anyone could understand what it's like to be pregnant with a miracle baby, it was her. Isn't it nice how God puts friends in our life that can understand what we are going through and be an encouragement to us? I'm sure Mary was happy to have someone to talk to that could relate to her situation.

Mary is a great example of someone who has faith. She believed God when the angel told her she was going to give birth to the Messiah. She didn't question Him or get upset about her circumstances. She didn't care what everyone else would think about her. She followed God. Because Mary had faith, God was able to use her.

♦ LET'S TALK

How would you describe Mary?

Why do you think God chose Mary to be the mother of Jesus?

How do you think Mary felt when the angel spoke to her and told her she would have a baby?

How is God able to use you?

★ PRAYER ★

Lord, help us to have the faith we need to trust Your plan for our lives with our whole heart. Use us to serve You for all of our days.

♦ FAMILY TIME ACTIVITIES

- Tell a story about a friend that God put in your life for encouragement.

- Make a Mary ornament for your Christmas tree. Mix 1 cup salt with 2 cups flour and 1 cup water. Knead for 10 minutes. You can take turns kneading and talk about the time that Mary had to wait while Jesus was growing inside her. Roll the dough out ¼ inch thick. Print and cut out the silhouette on Appendix A. Lay it on top of the dough. Use a toothpick or another pointed object to cut the silhouette out of the dough. Carefully place on a greased baking sheet and bake for 2 hours at 325 degrees. Once it is done baking and has cooled down, you can paint it or leave it as is. Put a ribbon through the hole at the top and hang it on your tree to remember how God was able to use Mary and how she had great faith.

- Read *Mary- The Mother of Jesus* by Carine MacKenzie.

- Sing or watch on YouTube "Hallelujah (Light Has Come)" by BarlowGirl.

10 Joseph

DECEMBER

A CLOSER LOOK

Did you know that in all of the Scripture passages that mention Joseph, he never says a word? What are recorded are his actions. We know that Joseph was a carpenter (Matthew 13:55). We also know from Mark 6:3 that Joseph passed on his trade to Jesus. It was customary in those days for a father to pass on his trade to his son(s).

Matthew 1:1 gives us Joseph's lineage, tracing his ancestry back to David. He was of the royal line. At this point, he was betrothed to Mary, but the marriage ceremony had not happened yet. Ancient Jewish weddings were much different from modern Western weddings. They began when the parents of the bride and groom arranged a marriage contract, where the groom's family paid the bride's family a price. Next was called the betrothal period, which could last up to a year. The couple was considered legally married during this period, but they did not live together. To break the contract in this period required a divorce decree. Next would come the wedding ceremony, and finally, the marriage would be consummated.[21]

During the betrothal period, Joseph discovered Mary was pregnant with a child that wasn't his. He was honorable and wanted to divorce Mary quietly without much public shame. However, an angel came to him in a dream and told him to take her as his wife and raise the child and name Him Jesus. Joseph obeyed without any question.

After Jesus was born and the wise men had presented their gifts to Him, God sent another angel to Joseph in a dream and told him to flee to Egypt for safety from Herod (Matthew 2:13). We don't know how long they stayed down in Egypt, but eventually Herod died and his orders to take Jesus' life were no longer standing. A third angel came in a dream and told Joseph they were safe to return to Nazareth (Matthew 2:20).

In all three encounters with the angel, we see one common theme in Joseph's response. He doesn't question; he just obeys in his actions and does what the angel commands.

Joseph is mentioned again when Jesus is twelve years old. Luke 2:41 tells us that every year Joseph would take his family up to Jerusalem to celebrate Passover. (Again, we see his devoutness to following the commands of God.) As they were heading home, Jesus stayed behind in the temple and was found three days later by His parents (Luke 2:50).

That is the last reference to Joseph found in Scripture. Scholars believe that Joseph died sometime between Jesus being twelve years old and His beginning of ministry around the age of thirty.[22] The strongest evidence of Joseph's death comes at the crucifixion. Jesus, as He is dying, asks John to take care of His mother (John 19:26-27). It was His responsibility to take care of her, and He was passing it on to John. If Joseph had still been alive, there would have been no need for Jesus to find someone to care for her.[23]

There is an old cliché that says, "Actions speak louder than words." This is true for Joseph. Through his actions, we can see that he was a man of integrity, a person of sound moral character, and that he walked upright and righteous before God.

Read Matthew 1:18-25

 **DAILY DEVOTION**

Joseph was highly respected, had great integrity, and was betrothed to Mary. When you are betrothed, you are considered husband and wife; you just don't live together until after the wedding. Life was going pretty well for Joseph until one day his beautiful wife-to-be informed him that she was pregnant. I am sure Joseph was devastated. After all, he knew he was not the father.

In those days, Mary could have been stoned to death for getting pregnant before her wedding. Joseph was such a kind man, though, that he decided to divorce her quietly without causing a scene. He didn't become angry or spiteful, he didn't yell and throw things, he decided to take the high road. It is not very often that we see people act honorably when they are wronged. But Joseph did.

Then one day an angel appeared to Joseph in a dream and said, "Joseph, son of David, do not be afraid to take Mary as your wife; for the Child who has been conceived in her is of the Holy Spirit. She will bear a Son; and you shall call His name Jesus, for He will save His people from their sins" (Matthew 1:20-21).

Joseph listened to the angel and took Mary for his wife and became a father to Jesus. He acted in faith, and God was able to use him mightily because of it. Did you know the Bible never mentions what Joseph said, it only mentions what he did? He is a true example of someone whose actions speak louder than words.

🧍 LET'S TALK

What character qualities do you see in Joseph?

What does the phrase "actions speak louder than words" mean?

What did Joseph's actions say about him?

What do your actions say about you?

★ PRAYER ★

Lord, help us to have a servant's heart. Help us to be kind and loving in everything we say and do, so that when people see us, they see You!

⚐ FAMILY TIME ACTIVITIES

- Tell a story about a time someone's words did not match his actions.

- Print out the "Joseph Award" in Appendix B. Have someone decorate it. Every night at dinner talk about someone in the family whose actions spoke louder than words and put the Joseph Award in front of his place setting for the evening. The next night, the person with the Joseph Award gets to pick the new person who gets it. They must give a specific example of something that happened that day before giving it to the new person.

- Read the page on Joseph in *Voices of Christmas* by Nikki Grimes.

- Sing "Good Christian Men Rejoice."

DECEMBER 11 Gabriel

A CLOSER LOOK

Angels played an important role in predicting and announcing the birth of Christ, specifically the angel Gabriel. He is one of only two angels named in the Bible (the other being Michael the Archangel[24]). There are a lot of misunderstandings about angels, and so it is important to examine Scripture to know what is true.

Gabriel appeared in four different passages in the Bible. (He also appeared in the book of Tobet in the Apocrypha along with Raphael and a few other named angels,[25] but for the purposes of this devotion we are focusing on the protestant canon only.) The first time Gabriel appeared was to the prophet Daniel, in Daniel 8:16. Daniel had just seen a vision that he was unable to interpret. Gabriel appeared to him as a man. He instantly struck fear into Daniel, who fell prostrate on the ground before him. Gabriel revealed details about the vision/prophecy that Daniel just saw, which had to deal with the end times (8:19).

Gabriel is mentioned for the second time in the next chapter. Daniel was praying to God, asking for details about the end of the seventieth year of captivity for the Jews in Babylon (9:2). Gabriel appeared during the prayer, arriving swiftly (9:21). This time, instead of coming to interpret a vision, Gabriel was bringing a revelation. This prophecy is called the seventy weeks prophecy (9:24-27). It contained information about the end times and included details about the coming Messiah. It said in verse 26 that "The anointed one would be put to death" (Anointed One is a reference to the Messiah). Both of these appearances occurred in the mid-500s B.C.,[26] hundreds of years before Jesus was born.

In Luke 1:11-20, Gabriel is mentioned for the third time. This passage describes his appearance to Zacharias in the temple. His presence scared Zacharias. This time, he told Zacharias that his wife Elizabeth would conceive and they would have a child. In response to Zacharias' doubt, Gabriel says, "I am Gabriel, who stands in the presence of God, and I have been sent to speak to you and to bring you this good news" (Luke 1:19). We find out that Gabriel stands in the presence of God, so the revelations that he brings can be trusted!

The last time that Gabriel is mentioned in the Bible is to Mary in Luke 1:26-38. He appears announcing that she will give birth to the Messiah. She is startled (just like Daniel and Zacharias), and he tells her to not be afraid, that she has found favor in the sight of God, and that she was chosen to give birth to Jesus.

In studying these different passages about Gabriel, we find out more about him and his job: When he appears to humans, he has the form of a man. He sits in the presence of God. He is an angel that is assigned to bring revelations not previously known. The revelations that he brings are big news that deal with the end of time and salvation for humanity.

Scholars think it is possible that Gabriel was the angel who appeared in the dreams of Joseph and the wise men, but since his name is not mentioned, we do not know for sure. What we do know is that Gabriel is obedient to God.

| Read | Luke 1:8-20 |
| | Luke 1:26-38 |

DAILY DEVOTION

Do you believe in angels? Sometimes it is hard to believe that angels are real because we have never seen one. However, there is an angel named Gabriel who played a very important role in the Christmas story. Gabriel was the angel who delivered the news to Zacharias that Elizabeth was going to have a baby. He was also the angel who told Mary she was going to have Jesus. Gabriel was God's messenger. How perfect is it that God used something supernatural like an angel to announce the miraculous birth of His Son?

The only things we know about Gabriel's character is that he is obedient to God and that he speaks the truth. In Luke 1:19, Gabriel says that he stands in the presence of God. It is obvious that God trusts him, especially since he was assigned to deliver the most important news mankind has ever heard.

Gabriel appeared one other time in the Bible in the book of Daniel. In Daniel 8:15, we get the only clue to how Gabriel looked. It says, "And behold, standing before me was one who looked like a man." Usually people think of angels as having wings and halos. We know some angels in the Bible have wings, but in this instance, Gabriel appears looking like a man. Even looking like a man, Gabriel had to tell Zacharias, Mary, and Daniel to not be afraid of him. How would you feel if an angel suddenly appeared in front of you?

LET'S TALK

What was Gabriel's job in the Bible?

What do we know about Gabriel's character?

Why do you think Mary and Joseph were frightened when they first saw Gabriel?

Why do you think God used an angel to tell Mary and Joseph about Jesus?

★ PRAYER ★

Lord, we desire to follow You.
Give us boldness to speak Your truths to those around us.

FAMILY TIME ACTIVITIES

- Watch the part of the movie "The Nativity Story" where the angel Gabriel appears to Mary.

- Give every member of your family a piece of paper and markers/crayons. Have everyone draw a picture of what they think Gabriel looks like. No one is allowed to see any of the other drawings until the very end. At the end, have everyone reveal their drawings and talk about why they chose to draw Gabriel that way.

- Read the page on Gabriel in *Voices of Christmas* by Nikki Grimes.

- Sing "Angels We Have Heard on High."

DECEMBER 12 Jesus of Nazareth

A CLOSER LOOK

No one has had more of a profound impact on humanity and history than Jesus. But what do we really know about Him beyond what we have learned in Sunday school? The Gospels give us some historical and biographical clues. Extra-biblical writers such as Josephus give us a few more. However, we will never know everything about Jesus' life on earth. John 21:25 says, "Jesus did many other things as well. If every one of them were written down, I suppose that even the whole world would not have room for the books that would be written."

The Gospels do give us some great details about His birth, His ministry years, and His final weeks on earth before His ascension. Matthew 1-2 and Luke 1-2 focus on His birth. Most scholars believe that Christ was born sometime between 6-4 B.C. They came up with this date based on the timing of the death of Herod the Great (It is believed that Herod died before an eclipse in 4 B.C.). There is a two year window because Herod ordered the death of all babies in Bethlehem under the age of two.

After being born, Jesus spent some time with His family in Egypt until Herod died. As His family made their way back home, they avoided Jerusalem and decided to settle in Nazareth. This is where Jesus grew up.

We have one mention of Jesus between the birth account and the launch of His ministry around the age of thirty. In Luke 2:41-51,

He was twelve years old and went with His parents to Jerusalem to celebrate the Passover. While His parents returned to Nazareth, He stayed behind in the temple. He conversed with the teachers there and amazed them with His knowledge and answers. From this passage we find out that He was an obedient child and continued to grow in wisdom and stature as He matured. Also important to note is that He grew in favor with man and God. He was pleasing to God with His actions, but He also pleased the people around Him. During this time, He learned to be a carpenter as a trade from Joseph (Mark 6:2-3).

The next major mark in His life was when His ministry began at the age of thirty (Luke 3:23). He was baptized by John the Baptist (Matthew 3:13-16, Luke 3:21-22). Scholars put this time period between 26 and 29 A.D. Luke 3:1 provides pretty specific details about when this event occurred; during the fifteenth year of the reign of Tiberius as emperor of Rome. Tiberius was adopted by Caesar Augustus as his heir. He died in 14 A.D.[27] Tiberius assumed the throne after this. The fifteenth year of his reign would have been 29 B.C., the year that Christ started His public ministry.

After being baptized, He went into the wilderness to be tempted by Satan. He was tempted, but did not give in (Matthew 4:1-11). After this, He returned to Galilee and attended a wedding (John 2:1-12). At this wedding, they ran out of wine. Jesus took water and turned it into wine. This was His first miracle. He would go on for the next three years in His ministry; teaching, healing, and performing miracles for groups big and small. We know that His ministry was at least three years long because three separate Passovers are mentioned in the book of John (John 2:23; 6:4; 11:55).

The final week of His life was spent in Jerusalem. He came in triumphantly on a donkey (Matthew 21:7; John 12:14). He cleansed the temple (Matthew 21:17-23) and healed many people. He had one last meal (Matthew 26:17-30; Mark 14:12-25; Luke 22:7-20) with His disciples and was betrayed by Judas (Luke 22:47-52). He was tried illegally by the Sanhedrin (Jewish High Court – Matthew 26:57-67) and brought before Pilate, who ordered Him crucified (Matthew 27:11-26). He died on the cross (Matthew 27:27-56; Mark 15:21-38; Luke 23:26-49; John 19:16-37). He was buried in a tomb (Matthew 27:57-60) and then rose again three days later (Matthew 28:1-10). He spent another forty days on earth appearing to more than five hundred people (1 Corinthians 15:6) before He returned back to Heaven (Acts 1:1-8).

Scholars believe that Jesus died in either 30 A.D. or 33 A.D.[28] They base this around several textual clues in the Bible. The first is that He died on a Friday (Matthew 27:62; Mark 15:42; Luke 23:54; John 19:42) and it was near Passover (Matthew 27:62; Mark 15:42; Luke 3:54; John 19:42). Between the years A.D. 29 (the year that Jesus started His ministry) and A.D. 36 (the last year that Pilate was proconsul of Judah), there were only two years that had Passovers occur on Friday: Friday, April 7, A.D. 30, or Friday, April 3, A.D. 33.[29] Since it has been established that Jesus' ministry was at least three years long, the A.D. 30 date is not viable. It seems the best date for the crucifixion is the A.D. 33 date. There is much more that could be written about Christ from just reading small chunks of the Gospels. However, most of that information falls outside the course of this study. For more reading on Jesus, check out *One Perfect Life* by John Macarthur.

Read   Matthew 4:12-25

 **DAILY DEVOTION**

It is Christmastime. The stores are decked out in ribbons and tinsel. Christmas trees adorned in colorful lights and beautiful ornaments fill living rooms. Children have lists of what presents they want to receive, and everywhere you go there is music in the air. Although Christmastime is a wonderful time of year, many people have lost sight of the real reason we celebrate Christmas. You see, one lonely night there was a little Baby born, and because there was no room for His family to stay in, He was wrapped in cloth and placed in a trough where animals eat. That Baby, born to a young mother and lying in a lowly manger, would grow up to be the greatest Man who ever lived.

His name is Jesus, and He is the real reason we celebrate Christmas.

The Bible tells us a little bit about Jesus' life growing up. We know that He was perfect and never sinned. Not even once! We know that when He was twelve years old He went to the temple with His parents to celebrate Passover. After it was over, His parents headed back to Nazareth and did not realize Jesus was not with them. He had stayed at the temple and was talking with all the teachers there, amazing them with His answers to their deep questions. He was very wise, even as a young boy.

The Bible doesn't tell us anything else about His childhood. The next time Jesus is mentioned, He was about thirty years old, and

His cousin, John the Baptist, baptized Him in the Jordan River. After His baptism, Jesus went into the desert and didn't eat anything for forty days. He spent the time praying to God. Satan came to Him in the desert and tried to tempt Him, but Jesus resisted Satan.

After His time in the desert, Jesus attended a wedding and performed His first miracle by turning water into wine. He went on to perform many more miracles, healing sick people, and bringing them hope and joy through His stories that He would tell them.

Three years later, the Bible tells us that Jesus was killed on a cross. He died to pay the price for all of our sins. Thankfully, that's not the end of His story. Three days later, He rose from the dead just like He said He would. Through His life and death and resurrection, that little Baby lying in a manger made salvation available to all of us. Thank you, Jesus!

 LET'S TALK

Why do we celebrate Christmas?

What can you tell me about the life of Jesus?

Why is Jesus the greatest Man who ever lived?

★ PRAYER ★

Lord, we praise You for loving us so much that You sent Your Son Jesus to earth for us. Thank You for His life, death, and resurrection. Help us to always remember that Jesus is the real reason we celebrate Christmas.

👧 FAMILY TIME ACTIVITIES

- Play the mystery gift game. Ahead of time, take baby Jesus from a nativity set and place it in a box. Wrap the box many different times. You can even put the small box into bigger boxes and keep wrapping. Once ready, have the whole family sit in a circle. Tell your family that inside the box is the true meaning of Christmas. Start some music and pass the box in a circle. When the music stops, whoever is holding the box gets to start unwrapping it layer by layer. They keep unwrapping until the music starts again. Whoever has the box when it gets to the baby Jesus is the winner and gets to explain how Jesus is the reason for the season.

- Make a timeline of Jesus' life on a big piece of butcher paper. Have everyone draw pictures to go along with each event/date. Use the verses from the 'A Closer Look' section for a starting point.

- Read *Jesus and the Family Trip* by Arch books.

- Sing "Away in a Manger."

DECEMBER 13 Mary's Magnificat

A CLOSER LOOK

Mary, after finding out from Gabriel that she will give birth to the Messiah, heads off to see her cousin Elizabeth (Luke 1:39-45). As she approaches Elizabeth, Elizabeth's baby jumps inside her. Elizabeth tells Mary that she will be blessed because she is carrying the Messiah. In response to Elizabeth's statement and supernatural acknowledgement of her pregnancy, Mary bursts forth in a song of joy. This is actually the first of several recorded songs in the birth narrative. This song is called the Magnificat because of its Latin translation (Luke 1:46-55). The first line of verse 47 says, "*Magnificat animum mea Dominum*" which is translated "my soul magnifies the Lord."[30] So roughly this song could be called Mary's Magnification. The first part of the song expresses great praise to God from the depths of her soul (vs. 47-48). She is filled with great joy because God has been mindful of her and remembered her (vs. 48). She is full of humility, knowing that God is high and mighty (Isaiah 55:8-9) and did not have to choose her and yet He did. This brings great joy to her.

In her Magnificat, Mary describes some character traits of God. The first character trait that Mary expresses praise for is found in verse 49. She exclaims that God is mighty! The mighty one had done great things for her. Specifically, He had included her in His plans for the salvation of humanity by choosing her to be the mother of Christ. In verse 51, she affirms that He has done mighty deeds with His arm.

The next thing she praises God for is His holiness (Luke 1:49). She says His name is holy! Holiness is the idea that something is set apart. God is set apart from sin[32]. His holiness expresses itself in ways that don't make sense to humans. We generally treat the lowly with less respect than those who have prestige. His holiness keeps Him from showing partiality to the rich over the poor, and for that Mary is thankful. In several lines of the Magnificat, she shows how He looks out for those with less. In verse 52, she mentions how He has brought up the humble. In verse 53, she mentions that He has filled up those who are hungry, while sending the rich away. In verses 54 and 55, He has remembered to help His servant Israel, as He had promised to Abraham and those who had come after him.

She praises God for being a God of mercy. Mercy couples closely with the idea of grace in Scripture. Grace is getting what we do not deserve, and mercy is not getting what we do deserve. For instance, we get the grace of God by having a gift of salvation offered to us. Mercy is shown by us not having to pay the price demanded for our sins.

In verse 50, Mary is thankful that God shows mercy to those who fear Him. Fear is not the idea of being afraid but more of reverence and awe. Mary notes that this mercy is not limited to just one person, but is extended from generation to generation. In verse 54, she is thankful for the mercy that God has shown to Israel throughout the generations by remembering His promises to their forefather Abraham. God, on many occasions in the Old Testament, became angry with the Jews because they abandoned Him and started following other gods. Yet He would show mercy on them and bring them back to Him time after time. The whole book of Judges is an example of God's mercy as the Jews repeated this cycle seven times in just that one book!

What we see in the Magnificat is Mary offering up a song of praise and thanksgiving to God for what He had done, from the depths of her soul. She was praising Him with everything that she had. We are commanded to bring praise and worship before God just like Mary did (Psalm 150:1-6). How can you bring praise to God today? What are you thankful for that He has done? Tell Him!

Read   Today's reading is in the devotion.

 **DAILY DEVOTION**

Do you like singing praises to God? What are your favorite praise songs to sing? There is a special song of praise that Mary sings in Luke chapter 1. It is called Mary's Magnificat. At the time of this song, Mary was pregnant and on her way to visit her cousin Elizabeth. Elizabeth was pregnant also. When she saw Mary coming, her baby jumped inside of her tummy and she was filled with the Holy Spirit. Elizabeth spoke blessings over Mary. This was so special to Mary that her heart overflowed with thanks and she sang her song of praise to God. Read her Magnificat and see if you can count how many different things she praises God for:

Luke 1:46-55

[46] And Mary said:

"My soul exalts the Lord,

[47] And my spirit has rejoiced in God my Savior.

[48] "For He has had regard for the humble state of His bondslave;

For behold, from this time on all generations will count me blessed.

[49] "For the Mighty One has done great things for me;

And holy is His name.

[50] "AND HIS MERCY IS UPON GENERATION AFTER GENERATION

TOWARD THOSE WHO FEAR HIM.

[51] "He has done mighty deeds with His arm;

He has scattered *those who were* proud in the thoughts of their heart.

[52] "He has brought down rulers from *their* thrones,

And has exalted those who were humble.

⁵³ "HE HAS FILLED THE HUNGRY WITH GOOD THINGS;

And sent away the rich empty-handed.

⁵⁴ "He has given help to Israel His servant,

In remembrance of His mercy,

⁵⁵ As He spoke to our fathers,

To Abraham and his descendants forever."

How many praises did you count? Have you ever felt so over-whelmed by God's goodness that you couldn't help but sing of His praise?

 ## LET'S TALK

Why do you think Mary sang the Magnificat?

In verse 49, Mary sings, "For the Mighty One has done great things for me." What great things has God done for you?

What do you praise God for?

★ PRAYER ★

Lord, we praise You for all that You have done for us. You give us life. You love us with an unending love. You know our every need and care about every detail of our lives. You alone are worthy of our praise!

🧍 FAMILY TIME ACTIVITIES

- Create a family Magnificat, writing out a song of specific praises to God. Post it somewhere prominent in your house where it can be a reminder of God's faithfulness towards your family.

- Play the praise game! Sit in a circle and pick a starting person. That person will say something that he praises God for. Then the next person says something he praises God for. Keep taking turns in a circle. When someone accidentally repeats a praise that has already been said or takes more than five seconds to think of a praise, he is out. The last person left praising is the winner. (But really everyone is a winner for having an attitude of praise!)

- Read *Let the Whole Earth Sing Praise* by Tomie de Paola.

- Sing your favorite praise song together. Our family loves the song "Mighty to Save."

DECEMBER 14 Zacharias' Prophecy

 **A CLOSER LOOK**

A miracle happened in Zacharias' life! He and his wife were old, and they had no children. Gabriel had come to visit them to let them know that they were going to have a child in their old age. Zacharias was doubtful and had his speech taken away for the whole pregnancy as a sign from God. When the child was born, they named him John, and Zacharias regained his speech. The first thing he said was a song of praise towards God. He uttered these words while filled with the Holy Spirit, and so they also contained some prophetic words about John's future. His song is recorded in Luke 1:67-80.

Zacharias starts out in verse 68 praising God for His willingness to come to His people and redeem them. *Redeem* refers to the costly salvation that He would make available to all people. In verses 69 and 70, Zacharias says that this redemption will come from the house of David. Jesus was from the line of David. This part of the song is anticipating the Messiah.

Verse 72 states that the Messiah would deliver people from their enemies. While it may be easy to think that this is referring to political or social enemies, this is more of a reference to Satan. He seeks to destroy followers of God in any way that he can (1 Peter 5:8).

Next, Zacharias remembers how God kept the covenant to Abraham as he continues his song of praise in verses 73-75. Since we are freed from the threat of enemies, we are now able to worship Him without fear and in righteousness for all the days of our lives. Christ bought our freedom on the cross with His life. We are delivered so that we might serve Him. We were given freedom so that we might accomplish a purpose, which, in this case, is the worship of God and living a life dedicated towards Him (1 Corinthians 6:19-20).

In the last section of the passage, Zacharias prophesies over his son. In verse 76, he calls his son the prophet of the Most High. This is huge! Israel has not had a prophet from God in over four hundred years[32]! John was to go on to prepare the way for the Lord (Isaiah 40:3-5). John was to prepare the way for Christ to come and bring knowledge of salvation (through Himself —see John 14:6), and they can have forgiveness of sins because of what Christ was going to do. Verse 78 tells us that God is merciful; in fact, He is full of tender mercies. He didn't have to send Christ as atonement, and yet He did.

The last verse of the song is filled with images of light and dark. The Bible uses images of light to convey truth and to represent God. Here, Christ is represented as the sun rising, bringing the truth of salvation. Those living in darkness haven't heard the truth of Christ, and because of this, they live in the shadow of death (sin leads to death – Romans 6:23). Zechariah's prophecy is a song of great praise to God and one that offers a portrait of how God works on our behalf: giving us mercies we don't deserve. Thank God for the mercies He gives to us!

Read   Luke 1:67-80

DAILY DEVOTION

Remember when Gabriel appeared to Zacharias and told him that his wife would have a baby? Zacharias questioned this information and had his voice taken away. For nine whole months Zacharias was not able to speak. Eight days after John the Baptist was born, Zacharias miraculously regained his voice. I'm sure he had a lot of things he wanted to say, wouldn't you? But the very first words out of his mouth were praises to God. His heart was overflowing and the Bible says he was "filled with the Holy Spirit." He sang praises to God for coming to redeem His people, for salvation, and for following through on His promises.

Then something really special happened. Because he was filled with the Holy Spirit, Zacharias began to prophesy over baby John. He told John that he would be a prophet of God. This was major news because it had been over four hundred years since Israel last had a prophet of God. He also told John that he would prepare the way for the Lord.

All of these things that Zacharias sang about came true! John the Baptist was a prophet for God, and he did prepare the way for Jesus. This news makes me want to sing praises to God too!

🚶 LET'S TALK

What would be the first words out of your mouth if you couldn't speak for nine months?

What is so special about Zacharias' song of praise?

How do you think everyone else reacted when Zacharias suddenly regained his voice and announced that John would be a prophet?

⭐ PRAYER ⭐

Lord, may we be like Zacharias and sing Your praise!
Let Your praise always be on our lips.

🚶 FAMILY TIME ACTIVITIES

- Try to get a feel for how Zacharias felt by playing the "no talking" game. See who can last the longest without talking. You must use hand signals and gestures to communicate. To make it harder, try to do something together without talking, like making dessert or playing a board game.

- Put your own tune to Zacharias' song in Luke 1:67-80. If you have any musical family members, have them compose a song and play it. If you do this, we would love to hear it. Feel free to post a video on our Facebook page https://www.facebook. com/SimpleLifeAbundantLife with the hash tag #Zecharias-song.

- Read the first chapter called "A Surprise for Zacharias" from *The Lion Storyteller Christmas Book* by Bob Hartman and Krisztina Kallai Nagy.

- Sing "Go Tell it on the Mountain."

15 The Census

DECEMBER

A CLOSER LOOK

"In those days Caesar Augustus issued a decree that a census should be taken of the entire Roman world. (This was the first census that took place while Quirinius was governor of Syria.) And everyone went to their own town to register." Luke 2:1-3

These verses contain the start to the traditional Christmas story. They also contain one of the hardest parts of the birth narrative for some to accept. The controversy surrounds the dating of the census decree and when Quirinius was governor of Syria. Most scholars believe that Jesus was born sometime between 6 and 4 B.C. Quirinius didn't become governor of Syria until sometime around A.D. 6[33]. Josephus records a census taking place in Syria in A.D. 6-7[34]. This is where the confusion arises; the dates, on the surface, don't match up. However, the differences can be reconciled.

Publius Sulpicius Quirinius (also called by his Greek name, Cyrenius) was a Roman Senator[35] who was campaigning against a group of people called the Homonadensians[36] in the area of Syria from about 12-2 B.C. So while he was later proclaimed as the governor of the new Roman province, he was in the area when Jesus was born. The Greek word used by Luke for governor in Luke 2:2 can also help shed some light on his role in this area. The word is *hegemoneuo*, which can be translated governor but has a more general meaning of "to be leading or in charge of[37]." So while he might not have the official title of governor from Rome, he was very much in charge of the area acting as the military governor.

The construction of verse 2 helps to provide a few clues. While it does say that this is the first census while Quirinius was governor, it could probably be better translated that this was the census before the census of Quirinius. Scholars N.T. Wright and Harold Hoehner have done some interesting research in this textual translation. N.T. Wright argues that *prōtos* not only means "first" but also can mean "before" (cf. John 1:15; 15:18)[38]. Harold Hoehner suggested that the passage should read, "This census was before that [census] when Quirinius was governor of Syria.[39]" Luke makes reference to the census of Quirinius because it was so well known; it was *the census*. However, he was differentiating the census mentioned in verse 1 and the census that sent Joseph and Mary back to Bethlehem.

Others find it hard to believe that the Romans would order so many people to return to their ancestral homelands to register for the census (Luke 2:3-5). Luke tells us that when the census was declared, Joseph left and took Mary with him to register in Bethlehem, the ancestral homeland of his forefather David. A papyrus was found in Egypt that records a very similar situation. An edict was issued by the Roman Governor of Egypt, G. Vibius Maximus. In the record, the author states, *"since the enrollment by households is approaching, it is necessary to command all who for any reason are out of their own district to return to their own home, in order to perform the usual business of taxation..."*[40] The same record also records that a man took his family to register with him[41]. This edict contains the exact situation that Joseph and Mary found themselves in. There was a census order of the empire (and there are quite a few recorded census' of the Empire over different periods[42]), and Joseph and Mary returned to his ancestral hometown of Bethlehem to register in the census. Joseph and Mary obeyed the authorities and went south. God used the census to bring the couple south in fulfillment of prophecy (Micah 5:2). While it may seem that Luke messed up his chronology of the birth narrative, there are explanations to explain the perceived discrepancies. Luke's history can be trusted.

Read   Luke 2:1-3

 **DAILY DEVOTION**

Did you know there are over 316 million people living in America? In order to find out that number, the American government had to perform a census. A census is when the government counts how many people live in their country. In the United States, the government does a census every ten years. Today they can do the census through the mail by sending out letters and having everyone fill it out and send it back in.

In Luke chapter 2, when Caesar Augustus decided to take a census, it was not that easy. They did not have our modern day mail system and computers and printers. Back then, everyone had to travel to their ancestral homeland to be accounted for. This meant Mary and Joseph had to travel all the way from Nazareth to Bethlehem, about seventy miles. They did not have cars back then, so they probably traveled by foot or rode on animals.

The census is an important part of the Christmas story because in Micah 5:2 it was prophesied that Jesus would be born in Bethlehem. Mary and Joseph lived in Nazareth. God used the census to get Mary and Joseph to Bethlehem to have baby Jesus. In this way the prophecy was fulfilled.

The census probably felt really inconvenient to Mary and Joseph, but it was all part of God's plan. This is true for the events in your life too. You never know how God is going to use your current situation to fulfill His plan for your life.

🚶 LET'S TALK

What is a census?

How do you think Mary felt, being very pregnant and having to travel a long distance?

Why is the census mentioned in Luke 2 an important part of the Christmas story?

⭐ PRAYER ⭐

Lord, You are sovereign and in control. You know every person who has ever lived by name and you love us all.

♟ FAMILY TIME ACTIVITIES

- Take a census of your extended family (you can include as many extended family members and pets as you want). If you made the family tree listed in December 1's devotional activities, you can use that to count up how many people make up your family. Afterwards, say a prayer thanking God for your family.

- Print out a map of the United States or the world and color in the states/countries in which you have relatives. Try to get a global picture for how spread out your family is and then talk about how you would all travel to see each other if you didn't have a car. You can find maps to print at http://www.yourchildlearns.com/megamaps/print-world-maps.html.

- Read and do the search and find activities on the Nazareth and Bethlehem pages of the book *The Life of Jesus* by Tim Dowley.

- Sing "O Come all Ye Faithful."

DECEMBER 16 No Room at the Inn

 **A CLOSER LOOK**

At the beginning of time, in Genesis 3:15, God promised that the seed of the woman would crush the head of the serpent. This was the first mention of the promise of a coming Messiah. The Old Testament is filled with prophecies anticipating a coming Messiah. Finally, after thousands of years of waiting, He came in the form of a newborn baby.

However, that birth story we all know and love is not completely accurate to what the Bible says. Looking deeper at Luke 2:6-7 provides a guide to understanding what really happened the night Christ chose to make His entrance into the world. At the end of verse 5, Joseph and Mary are on their way to Bethlehem to register for the census. They arrived and Mary was not in labor as most retellings of the nativity story would have you believe. In fact, they were there for a period of time before she went into labor. Verse 6 states; "While they were there, the days were completed for her to give birth," showing that they were there for a period of time before labor began.

Another element of the story that is often misunderstood is the belief that there was no room for Mary and Joseph at the inn. They were not staying at a hotel. It is believed that they were staying at a relative's house[43]. The word for *inn* that is used here in the Greek by Luke is not a word that describes a business. The word is *kataluma*, which means guest room[44]. This was the same word he used when he was describing the room the Last Supper was held in. In fact, if he had wanted to say *inn*, there was a word for that. It is *pandeion*. This is the same word that is used for the inn found in the parable of the Good Samaritan[45].

Archeologists have excavated houses from around this time period in Bethlehem and have found that many of them have caves out back and underneath[46]. These areas were used to house the animals. Joseph and Mary most likely stayed at a relative's house, but because the relatives did not have a guest room available, they had to stay in the cave out back.

So while the stories that are heard about Jesus' birth might not match up with what Scripture says, the important part of the story is this: the Child who would be the hope of humanity and bring the offer of salvation to the world was born. That is what we celebrate at Christmas!

> # Read   Luke 2:6-7

 **DAILY DEVOTION**

Every time you hear the Christmas story, you imagine Mary and Joseph wandering around Bethlehem after their long journey from Nazareth, looking for a place for her to give birth. You picture them knocking on doors and the innkeepers sadly shaking their heads and saying, "Sorry, there are no rooms available." You picture Mary, in active labor, needing a place to rest and give

birth to baby Jesus. Finally, you picture one kind innkeeper gener-
ously giving permission for them to stay in his stable with the animals. We have these images in our heads because this is how the
Christmas story is portrayed in nearly every book, story, and movie.

What if I told you we are probably wrong in how we
imagine this scene? The Bible only gives us two verses describing what happened: "While they were there, the days were completed for her to give birth. And she gave birth to her firstborn son; and she wrapped Him in cloths, and laid Him in a
manger, because there was no room for them in the inn" (Luke 2:6-7).

Notice how it starts? **"While they were there, the time came
for the baby to be born".** From this verse we can see that they weren't
just arriving in Bethlehem, they had already been there for a while. Later on, verse 7 it says, **"there was no room for them in the inn".** The
word for *inn* actually means guest room. A guest room is an extra room
people have in their houses for guests to stay in. Mary and Joseph were
probably staying with relatives, and because there was no guest room
available in the house, they had to stay in the cave that the animals slept in.

Although most depictions of this story might not follow exactly what the Bible says, the truth still remains: Jesus Christ, our Savior, was born.

♦ LET'S TALK

How is this part of the story different than you imagined?

Where do guests stay when they come to visit you?

Why do you think God planned for there to be no room for Jesus in the house?

★ PRAYER ★

Lord, we know it was Your plan to have Jesus, the King of kings, born in such a humble way. Thank You that Jesus came to serve the poor and the needy, not just the rich and privileged.

♦ FAMILY TIME ACTIVITIES

- Talk about a time you travelled somewhere, and imagine what you would have done if you had no place to stay.

- Create your own picture book depicting the nativity story the way that it is written in the Bible.

- Read *Jesus is Born* by Rev. Jim Reimann.

- Read or sing the lyrics to the old hymn "No Room at the Inn" by Henry John Gauntlett.

DECEMBER 17 — The Manger

 **A CLOSER LOOK**

Luke 2:7 says, *"And she gave birth to her firstborn son; and she wrapped Him in cloths, and laid Him in a manger."* The Greek word for manger is *phatne* and literally means a crib or a manger[47]. Most of the time *phatne* is used in reference to a feeding trough for animals. Most first century houses excavated in Bethlehem had mangers in them. The houses usually had a main room where the family would sleep and then an area behind the main room where the family would store food and animals[48]; this sometimes could be a cave the house was attached to. The animals would be brought in at night and placed in that room for protection from theft and the elements[49]. Mangers (or feeding troughs) could be found in these rooms. These troughs wouldn't have been clean and nice like seen in most nativity sets. After all, animals eat out of them. Go visit a barn and look at the trough that the animals eat out of. Then imagine placing a newborn baby in that trough.

Have you ever wondered why Jesus chose to be born in such a humble place? Most modern birthing suites are wonders of technology. They are comfortable and convenient. Some even have Wi-Fi! While these places didn't exist in the first century, there were still much less humble places to be born. It is said that Herod's palace was visible from Bethlehem and only six miles down the road in Jerusalem. Why would the Creator of the Universe, when He took on human flesh, plan to be born in such humble circumstances when He could have been born in a palace?[50]

Isaiah 53 gives us a clue. This chapter presents the Messiah as the suffering servant. A humble beginning, such as being born where the animals are housed, leads into this idea of coming to suffer. Philippians 2:6-8 spells it out more clearly. Jesus *"who, although He existed in the form of God, did not regard equality with God a thing to be grasped, but emptied Himself, taking the form of a bond-servant, and being made in the likeness of men. Being found in appearance as a man, He humbled Himself by becoming obedient to the point of death, even death on a cross."* Christ chose to be born in humble circumstances because He was coming to be a servant. He humbled himself for our sakes, including being placed in a manger and dying a criminal's death.

Read   Luke 2:7

 **DAILY DEVOTION**

Have you ever seen a trough that animals eat out of? They are usually pretty dirty. They certainly are not fit for a newborn baby. And yet, this is where Mary and Joseph placed Jesus after His birth. Do you ever wonder why Jesus was born in a yucky, dirty, place fit for animals instead of a beautiful, clean palace fit for a king? Sure, we know that there was no room for Mary and Joseph inside, but considering that Jesus is God, you would think that special arrangements could be made! However, the circumstances of Jesus' birth are not an accident. He was meant to be born in a lowly cave and placed in a manger. It was part of God's plan.

But why?

Jesus came to earth with the purpose of paying the price for our sins through His death on the cross. He spoke about the importance of us serving one another in love. He proved these words with His actions. He was born the way a servant would be born and lived a life serving others all the way to His death and resurrection. The simple action of placing Him in a manger was an announcement to the world that He had come for everyone: the rich and the poor, the sick and the needy, for me and for you.

LET'S TALK

Would you want to sleep in a manger at night?

Why wasn't Jesus born in a palace?

What does it mean to be humble?

How can you serve others today?

⭐ PRAYER ⭐

Lord, our hearts are humbled at the thought of Your Son coming to earth to be a servant for us. Please help us to love and serve others the way You want us to.

FAMILY TIME ACTIVITIES

- Make a family plan to intentionally serve someone this week. It could be anything from cooking a dinner for a family that needs it, writing an encouraging note to someone struggling, or even offering to watch a weary mother's kids so she can have a couple of hours of rest (or Christmas shopping).

- Have one person in your family wash everyone's feet the way Jesus washed the disciple's feet in John 13. Afterwards talk about how it felt to serve and be served.

- Read *The Three Trees, A Traditional Folktale* by Elena Pasquali.

- Sing "Away in a Manger."

18 DECEMBER — The Shephards and Angels

A CLOSER LOOK

After Christ was born, Luke's narrative changes scenes and moves out into the hills around Bethlehem where shepherds kept watch over their sheep. It was not unusual for shepherds to be in the hills at any time of the year. A lot of the hills around Bethlehem were prime grazing land. Many of the lambs that were sacrificed in the temple actually came from these hills[51]. In Luke 2:9, the angel of the Lord appeared to these shepherds with some great news. When he appeared, the sky was full of brilliant light as the glory of God shone around them. This is one of the rare times that God chose to make His presence known.

An appearance like this is called the Shekinah Glory. Shekinah is an extra-biblical Hebrew word coined by rabbis that literally means "He caused to dwell.[52]" The Shekinah was a visible symbol of God's presence to His people[53]. Several times in the Old Testament, there were visible symbols of God's presence: As the Israelites were wandering in the wilderness, there was a cloud that would lead them by day and a pillar of fire that would lead them by night (Exodus 13:20-22). When the first temple was being dedicated by Solomon, the glory of God became visible as fire came down and consumed an offering and then the glory settled into the temple (2 Chronicles 7:1-3). In the future, when Christ is reigning on earth in the New Jerusalem, there will be no need for the moon or stars. The light of God's glory will provide light for all the people living there (Revelation 21:23-24).

The Greek word for angel is *aggelos* which is translated into English as *angel*, but has an actual meaning of messenger[54]. This angel had one of the biggest messages in the course of the history of \the world to deliver! The angel told the shepherds in verse 11, "For today in the city of David there has been born for you a Savior, who is Christ the Lord." This announcement has some huge theological implications. The first important word in the announcement is *Savior*. This comes from the Greek word *soter*, which has a meaning of savior or deliverer[55]. This word only appears one other time in the Gospels (John 4:42) when some men confess that Jesus is the Savior of the world. The concept of savior is further developed in other sections of the New Testament[56]. In Romans, Paul develops the concept of humanities sinfulness and our need for a savior. In Matthew, the angel Gabriel announces that Jesus would save the people from their sins (Matthew 1:21).

The next theologically important word is *Christ*. While some might think that Christ is Jesus' last name, it is actually a title. Christ is a transliteration of the Greek word *Christos*. This word means Anointed One[57] (Psalms 45:7) or Messiah[58]. The word can be traced back to Daniel 9:26. In this prophecy, Daniel says the Messiah would be cut off, or killed. This is one of many reference\ in the Old Testament to the coming Messiah of Israel.

The angel then calls the Jesus " Lord." The Greek word used here is *kurios*. *Kurios* can either mean lord or master in a generic sense[59]. It was mostly used to denote deity[60]. The word is adopted by New Testament authors to refer to God. They connect the word with the name of God, Jehovah, from the Old Testament. By making this proclamation, the angel is connecting the newborn child with the Creator of the Universe. He is ascribing to Him deity (Isaiah 9:6-7).

Next, the angel tells the shepherds how to find the newborn child. "You will find a baby wrapped in cloths and lying in a manger" (Luke 2:12). As the angel finishes saying this, a great number of angels burst forth onto the scene. Usually, when angels appear in the Bible, they appear in ones or twos. They rarely come in great multitudes. When they do, something big and glorious is happening. The multitude is called the heavenly host. Revelation 5:11 tells us that the number of angels in Heaven is "thousands times thousands and ten thousands by the thousands" (i.e. there are a whole lot of them). A company of this host is sent to make a proclamation. The angels bring praise to God in verse 14 by saying, "Glory to God in the highest, and on earth peace among men with whom He is pleased."

These words the angels proclaim contain another deep theological truth. In the King James Version of the Bible, the statement reads, "Peace on earth good will towards men." Many have confused this to mean that the angels are wishing peace to all mankind. (Peace being defined as tranquility and the absence of war[61]). However this is a wrong assumption. Peace here is talking about a relational position before God. God is holy and people are naturally sinners (see Romans 3:23). This makes us enemies of God (see Romans 5:10). However because Christ came and died for us, bringing forgiveness of sins, peace has been restored between God and people that have put their faith in Christ (Romans 5:1-2). So when the angels proclaim "peace on earth goo\d will towards men," they are referring to the peace that Christ will bring in the relationship between God and man.

After this, the angels returned to Heaven. The shepherds were, no doubt, standing in awe at the news and sights they had just taken in. They decided to go find this baby. We are not told how they knew which guest room to go and visit. Perhaps they were guided there, or since Bethlehem was a pretty small town, they had known that Mary had arrived pregnant and figured out that she was the one that had given birth. They arrived and found Jesus just as the angels had told them they would, wrapped up and lying in a manger. They told as many people as they could the good news of the birth of the Messiah, and people were amazed at what they were saying.

Have you ever wondered why the angels made the announcement of the birth to the shepherds and not someone else? It fits in with the whole theme of the birth narrative. Christ was born in humble conditions, not to wealthy parents. The shepherds were of lowly social order. To have the announcement given to someone else would not fit the narrative. The birth announcement provides a very exciting part of the birth narrative. In dramatic fashion, with theologically rich words, the angels announced the birth of the Messiah to the shepherds and the world!

Read   Luke 2:8-20

⌂ DAILY DEVOTION

After Jesus was born, an angel appeared to some shepherds that were living in the fields near Bethlehem. The Bible says that "the glory of the Lord shone around them, and they were terrified." Can you imagine? Here they are, merely shepherds, watching their sheep like they do every night, and all of a sudden a huge light floods the field and an angel appears out of nowhere. I would be terrified too!

The angel tells them, "Do not be afraid. I bring you good news that will cause great joy for all the people. Today in the town of David a Savior has been born to you; he is the Messiah, the Lord. This will be a sign to you: You will find a baby wrapped in cloths and lying in a manger" (Luke 2:10-12).

After the angel gave his message, more angels appeared, and they all praised God. I'm sure the shepherds were speechless as they tried to comprehend what was happening.

After such a miraculous announcement, they knew that they had to go see this baby. I bet seeing a group of shepherds running into town looking for a baby lying in a manger was enough to make the neighbors start to question what was going on. The shepherds started telling their story to anyone who would listen, and the Bible says, "All who heard it were amazed" (Luke 2:18).

⸫ LET'S TALK

The shepherds were some of the poorest people in town. Why do you think God chose for the angels to appear to them?

How would you feel if you were one of the shepherds and all

of a sudden angels appeared to you?

What did the angel mean when he said that "a Savior has been born to you"?

The shepherds told everyone that would listen about Jesus. How can you tell your friends about Jesus?

★ PRAYER ★

Lord, help us to be more like the shepherds by seeking You with our whole hearts and telling everyone we know about You.

FAMILY TIME ACTIVITIES

- Read *The Legend of the Candy Cane* by Lori Walburg (for school-aged children) or *J is for Jesus: The Sweetest Story Ever Told* by Crystal Bowman (for toddlers). Talk about how you can use a candy cane to tell others about Jesus.

- Re-enact with your facial expressions all the emotions that the shepherds experienced. Start with fear, then surprise, awe, and excitement. You can even take some fun family pictures with everyone making the different facial expressions and print them out along with the corresponding verses to hang on your refrigerator (or frame).

- Read *The Crippled Lamb* by Max Lucado.

- Sing "It Came Upon the Midnight Clear."

19 The Magi (Wise Men)

DECEMBER

 **A CLOSER LOOK**

The wise men are an integral part of the birth narrative. They are only mentioned in Matthew 2:1-12. Verse 1 states that the Magi were from the lands in the east. Many scholars think that they were Persian and came from an area around Babylon. The word *magi* was originally used to describe a certain people group who studied the stars in that area of the world[62]. If they were from the area around Babylon, it would be easy to imagine that they were looking for a sign in the heavens declaring the birth of the King. Between 605 and 587 B.C., the Babylonian Empire had conquered Judah and Jerusalem. In the conquest, Nebuchadnezzar had deported large amounts of the Jewish population and settled them in Babylon. One of them, Daniel, distinguished himself among the others taken captive and was put in the service of the king. Then, he performed such an impossible task that the king rewarded him by making him governor of the province of Babylon and the chief of the wise men (Daniel 2:48; 5:11). Daniel was put into a unique position to have an influence on the magi. Scholars believe that because of this, he was able to share some of the Scriptures with the magi. It is believed that he shared with them what is called the star prophecy. Found in Numbers 24:17, the prophecy states: "*A star will come out of Jacob.*" This prophecy predicted the Messiah would come from Jacob (Israel) and be announced by a star. It was most likely because of this influence that, centuries later, the wise men knew to look up and search for signs in the sky for the birth of the King.

When they saw the star, they knew the Messiah had been born. They left for Jerusalem to see the King. They arrived in Jerusalem and caused a great ruckus. They knew the star had guided them there, but they needed more information to find the child. Herod was unaware of the birth, and he and his scholars had not seen a star. This provides something interesting to think about. What kind of star had the Magi seen but no one in Jerusalem saw? There have been many different explanations offered. Some people have suggested that it was a comet or meteor. Meteors are only visible for short periods of time because they burn up quickly in the atmosphere. It was a several month journey that the Magi had taken from Babylon to Jerusalem. It is five hundred miles directly from Jerusalem to Babylon, but they actually travelled nine hundred miles[63] because the trade roads were not direct. A meteor would not have stayed visible in the skies for that length of time. Others have suggested a comet (such as Halley's Comet). However, there are no recorded comets that were visible during the window of time that Christ was born. Still others have suggested a nova or supernova (stars that violently exploded) as the star. Again there are no recorded events like this during the time period, and people in Jerusalem would have been able to see that.

This leaves two possibilities: One is a conjunction between a planet and star or two planets. Johannes Kepler (a famous astronomer) plotted back in 1603 that there was a triple conjunction (the planets appeared to join in the sky three times that year) between Saturn and Jupiter in 7 B.C.[64]. A recent research documentary title *The Bethlehem*

Star suggested that the star was a conjunction between the planet Jupiter and the star Regulus in 3/2 B.C.[65]. This theory would work out because the conjunction would be visible to all, but only those looking for it would have known what they were looking at. Others have suggested that rather than a naturally occurring phenomenon, the star was actually another appearance of the Shekinah Glory, similar to the pillar, that guided the Israelites in the wilderness in Exodus 13:21. While the Bible doesn't specify what the star was, we do know it guided the Magi from the East to come and worship the newborn King!

Read   Matthew 2:1-12

 **DAILY DEVOTION**

The story of the wise men has always amazed me. Unlike the other characters in the nativity, an angel didn't appear to them and tell them about the birth of Jesus. They were not told to go and find Jesus. They made their own observation of the star in the sky and decided on their own to travel over nine hundred miles and to bring their finest gifts to a baby.

I wonder what kind of conversations those men had on their journey. They must have been waiting their whole lives to see that star appear in the sky. They must have been giddy at the thought of meeting the newborn King of the Jews. In fact, Matthew 2:10 says,

"They rejoiced exceedingly with great joy" when they saw the star. The pictures in the storybooks always make the wise men look so serious. However, I imagine them with huge smiles, laughing deep belly laughs, and full of joy.

Then there was King Herod. He was not joyful when he heard about the new King of the Jews. He tried to get the wise men to give him more information about Jesus' location, but God warned them in a dream to not return to Herod. They were faithful to obey God and took another way home.

These wise men knew Jesus was the King of kings and worthy of all praise even though He was just a baby. They were faithful in traveling nine hundred miles to see this baby for themselves and to worship Him. I'm sure they were tired and sore by the time they arrived in Bethlehem, but they let nothing stop them from worshiping the King. What a testimony! Sometimes it is hard for us to worship God, and we don't even have to leave our house. We should be more like the wise men and joyfully set aside time from our own lives to seek God and bring Him praise.

LET'S TALK

Why wasn't King Herod excited about the news of baby Jesus?

What character qualities do you see in the wise men?

Would you follow a star, traveling hundreds of miles, to worship Jesus? Why?

★ PRAYER ★

Lord, help us to seek You with the same dedication as the wise men. Fill us with exceeding joy. You are Lord and worthy of all our praise.

🧍 FAMILY TIME ACTIVITIES

- Cut some stars out of yellow construction paper and write out clues on them to different places within your house (or outside). Have the last clue lead to the baby Jesus from your nativity set. After the lesson, hand out the first clue to one of your kids and tell them they have to follow the stars to get to Jesus, just like the wise men did.

- Alternately, turn off some of the lights in the house and have one person hold a flashlight. Have your children journey through the house pretending to be the wise men looking for baby Jesus, following "the light" of the leader. You can have fun with this one and shine the light around the hallways and rooms, even outside, as the kids follow it. Have the light end up in the kitchen with the baby Jesus from your nativity set on the table with a fun snack. Rejoice that you found Jesus, just as the wise men did, and eat your treat together.

- Read *Song of the Stars: A Christmas Story* by Sally Lloyd-Jones.

- Sing "O Holy Night."

DECEMBER 20 The Magi's Gifts

A CLOSER LOOK

The Magi, after leaving Herod's palace, went to Bethlehem where they found Jesus. Matthew 2:11 says, "After coming into the house they saw the Child with Mary His mother; and they fell to the ground and worshiped Him. Then, opening their treasures, they presented to Him gifts of gold, frankincense, and myrrh."

These were amazing gifts to present to a poor family. These were gifts that were typically presented to kings and even offered to pagan gods in temples. It is recorded, that in 243 B.C., the King Seleucus II Callinius offered the same gifts to the pagan god Apollo at the temple in Miletus[66]. It was even prophesied in the book of Isaiah that the Messiah would have visitors who would come bringing gold and frankincense (Isaiah 60:6)[67].

The gold was of great value and would have paid the family's expenses for a while. Frankincense is incense that is burned, and myrrh is a perfume used to embalm dead people[68]. There are some who see some great theological significance in the choice of gifts brought to Christ: To bring Christ gold, was to acknowledge His kingship[69]. To bring frankincense, they were acknowledging His deity[70]. To bring myrrh, they were acknowledging the importance of His eventual death[71]. While this could have been the case, Scripture is silent on the meaning of the gifts. It just records that the gifts were brought.

The Magi came and visited Jesus with the sole purpose of worshiping Him. They travelled hundreds of miles to meet the King. They fell down before Him, worshiped Him, and presented Him gifts worthy of a king. They gave Him their very best.

| Read | Matthew 2:11 |

 **DAILY DEVOTION**

The wise men travelled a long way to bring Jesus their gifts. They brought Him gold, frankincense, and myrrh. How would you feel if you got those gifts for your birthday?

They may seem like strange gifts to give a baby, but that's because they are gifts for a king. Gold is a precious metal worth a lot of money. It was common back then to give gold to kings. Even today gold would be a rare and valuable gift to receive.

Frankincense is derived from a special tree and is used to make perfume and incense. Back then, frankincense would be burned in the temple to God. Maybe the wise men understood that Jesus was the Son of God.

Myrrh was the strangest gift of the three. Myrrh is a spice that was used to embalm dead people. It would help preserve the body and cover the stench. By giving Jesus myrrh, perhaps the wise men were acknowledging the importance of His death.

The wise men brought the very best they had and presented it to God as an act of worship. What can you give to God as an act of worship?

 **LET'S TALK**

What three gifts did the wise men give to Jesus?

Why did the wise men bring gifts?

If you could travel with the wise men and give a gift to Jesus, what would you give Him?

★ PRAYER ★

Lord, we give ourselves to You as a gift of worship. We love You because we are fearfully and wonderfully made in Your image.

👧 FAMILY TIME ACTIVITIES

- Just for fun, discuss as a family what three gifts you would give each other if money was not an object.

- What is the most valuable thing you own? Discuss as a family if that is something you would be willing to give to Jesus.

- Read the page on Balthasar in the book *Voices of Christmas*.

- Sing "The Little Drummer Boy."

21 DECEMBER Simeon and Anna

 **A CLOSER LOOK**

There are two interesting characters in the Luke account of the nativity story that are often left out of retellings. Simeon and Anna and can be found in Luke 2:21-39. This part of the narrative takes place forty days after the birth of Christ.

As was tradition, eight days after birth, Jesus was circumcised and given His name. Forty days after His birth, Mary and Joseph took Jesus with them to the temple in Jerusalem, so the family could complete the purification rituals (Leviticus 12: 6-8). They offered a pair of doves as a sacrifice to God in keeping with Old Testament traditions found in Leviticus 12:8. (This is one way that we know they were poor. They offered a sacrifice that could only be afforded by the poor; the rich would have offered bigger animals. This is also a sign that the Magi didn't arrive until Jesus was a child. If they had already been given the gold, frankincense, and myrrh, they could have afforded more expensive animals to sacrifice.)

The first person the family runs into on the way to the temple is Simeon. Verse 25 describes Simeon as a righteous and devout man. He was an older man, who was waiting around for a prophecy to come true. It was revealed to him by the Holy Spirit that he wouldn't die until he had seen the Messiah. The Holy Spirit nudged him one morning to go to the temple. As he was waiting, he saw the family arrive. He ran up to them and took Jesus in his arms and burst forth in praise to God in what is called the *Nunc Dimittis*[72], the fourth song of praise found in the birth narrative. "Now Lord, You are releasing Your bond-servant to depart in peace, according to Your word; For my eyes have seen Your salvation, which You have prepared in the presence of all peoples, A LIGHT OF REVELATION TO THE GENTILES, and the glory of Your people Israel" (Luke 2:29-32).

Joseph and Mary marveled at the words that Simeon offered. They were going to continue on their way, until Simeon pulled Mary aside. He offered her another prophecy. Simeon wasn't a prophet by trade, but under the influence of the Holy Spirit he was given divine revelation. In verse 34, he states, *"Behold, this Child is appointed for the fall and rise of many in Israel."* Those who fall or stumble are people who have rejected Jesus (1 Peter 2:8), and those who receive Him would be lifted up with Him (Ephesians 2:6). In verse 35, Simeon said that people's hearts would be revealed by their response to Him. Simeon then finished by stating that a sword would pierce Mary's soul. This was probably a reference to the grief that Mary would feel when she saw her Son executed (John 19:25).

After their encounter with Simeon, the family ran into Anna, who was a prophetess. She had been married for seven years and then her husband passed away. She was eighty-four years old. After her husband had died, she decided to dedicate herself to the service of the Lord instead of remarrying. It is believed that she actually lived in the temple and thus was able to dedicate herself completely to serving God[73]. When she saw the family, Luke 2:38 says, "She came up and *began* giving thanks to God, and continued to speak of Him to all those who were looking for the redemption of Jerusalem."

After completing everything required by the Law, the family returned to Nazareth. Luke leaves out a whole part of the story (the Magi coming and the family fleeing down to Egypt to escape Herod's wrath before returning to Nazareth). However this is not a mistake. Different eyewitnesses to the same event will record different details, and that is exactly what Matthew and Luke did. It is interesting that God used two more people, Anna and Simeon, that were outside the leadership caste to be witnesses of the Messiah. Further proof that Christ came to save all: men and women, rich and poor.

Read	Luke 2:25-38

 **DAILY DEVOTION**

When Jesus was a little over a month old, His family headed to Jerusalem for their purification rituals. They had to present a burnt offering and a sin offering in order for Mary to be considered ceremonially clean after giving birth. They were so poor that all they could offer were doves instead of lambs or bigger animals.

When they arrived in Jerusalem, a wise old man who loved God very much greeted them. His name was Simeon. Simeon was told by God that he would not die until he saw the Messiah. When Simeon saw baby Jesus, he took Him in his arms and said, "Sovereign Lord, as you have promised, you may now dismiss your servant in peace." (Luke 2:29). Then Simeon spoke blessings over Jesus.

Mary and Joseph also met another person when they were in Jerusalem. Her name was Anna. She was very old, and since her husband had died, she lived in the temple worshiping God day and night. She was a prophetess. That means God told her things that she would share with others. When she saw baby Jesus, she gave thanks to God and told everyone about Him.

Both Simeon and Anna were faithful to follow God. Both offered up praise to God for allowing them to see their Savior. Although they play only a tiny part in the nativity story, God put them there for a reason. It doesn't matter if you are young or old or rich or poor, God came to save us all!

LET'S TALK

What would you do if you saw baby Jesus out around town with His parents?

Why do you think Luke included Simeon and Anna in his telling of the Christmas story?

What is something we could learn from Simeon and Anna?

★ PRAYER ★

Lord, thank You for giving us examples of people, like Anna and Simeon, who worshiped You until their very last day.

⭑ FAMILY TIME ACTIVITIES

- Talk about people you know (or know of) that worship God faithfully the way Simeon and Anna did.

- Find some medium sized river rocks and paint words on them that describe God such as faithful, loving, perfect, etc. Find a place in your yard to place the rocks as a constant reminder of who God is in your lives.

- Read the pages on Simeon and Anna in the book *Voices of Christmas* by Nikki Grimes.

- Sing "God Rest You Merry, Gentlemen."

DECEMBER 22 Myths of the Christmas Story

*This day does not have an 'A Closer Look' section.

 **DAILY DEVOTION**

The Christmas story is one of the most famous Bible stories. Even people who are not Christians are usually familiar with all or parts of the story about Mary, Joseph, and Jesus. However, you may be surprised to find out that not everything we have heard about the Christmas story is true. Today we will talk about some of the myths we believe about the Christmas story and what the Bible really says.

Myth #1- Mary rode a donkey to Bethlehem.

Read Luke 2:4-5

Nowhere in Luke 2:4-5 does it say that Mary rode on a donkey to Bethlehem. What it does say is that Joseph traveled to Bethlehem with his pregnant wife.

THE TRUTH: We don't know what form of transportation they used to get there.

Myth #2 – There were animals present at Christ's birth.

Read Luke 2:7

Every picture book depicts animals peering at baby Jesus in the manger.

THE TRUTH: Luke makes no mention of animals being present at the birth. It just says that Jesus was laid in the manger (an indoor feeding trough for animals) in Luke 2:7.

Myth #3- The angels sang to the shepherds.

Read Luke 2:13-14

Traditional tellings of the Christmas story always includes the angels singing to the shepherds.

THE TRUTH: Nowhere in Luke 2 does it say that the angels sang. It says, "And suddenly there appeared with the angel a multitude of the heavenly host **praising God and saying**, 'Glory to God in the highest and on earth peace among men with whom he is pleased'" (Luke 2:13-14).

Myth #4 – Three kings arrive at the birth of Jesus after traveling a long distance on camels.

Read Matthew 2:1;11

This myth actually contains four myths:

- *The number:* The common assumption is that there were three wise men because the Magi presented three gifts.

THE TRUTH: In the Matthew passage (2:1-12), no numbers are given. In fact, all we know is that at least two and possibly more came.

- *They were kings:* The Magi are often referred to as kings like in the song "We Three Kings."

THE TRUTH: The Magi were not kings. They were astrologers or wise men presumably from the courts of a Persian king.

- *They arrived the night of the birth:* We always see pictures of the wise men at the birth of Jesus.

THE TRUTH: Matthew 2:11 states that they came to see the Child in a house. Jesus is not called an infant but a child. He is also in a house at this point, rather than a stable or cave. The Magi came at some point between His birth and age two, but were not present at the actual birth of Jesus.

- *They rode on camels:* The Magi are almost always pictured as riding on camels.

THE TRUTH: It is thought that Persian nobility rode on horses when traveling, but the Bible doesn't say for sure one way or the other.

(For more details, see 'A Closer Look' on December 19 and 20.)

Myth #5 – Jesus was born on December 25

Tradition states that Jesus was born on December 25.

THE TRUTH: We don't know the actual date Jesus was born. It wasn't until the 4th century A.D., that the Roman Catholic Church decreed that Christ's birth be celebrated on December 25. This date was originally a pagan holiday that coincided with the winter solstice. After reforms brought to the Roman Empire by Constantine, it seemed natural to pick that date. They replaced the pagan holiday with a Christian holiday. It is thought that His birth could have happened sometime between spring and fall because of a statement about the shepherds being in the fields at night in Luke 2:8.

LET'S TALK

Did any of these myths surprise you?

How do you think these myths came to be accepted as part of the Christmas story?

Do these myths change the true meaning of the story?

★ PRAYER ★

Lord, thank You for giving us Your Word.
Help us to always turn to it so we may know what is true.

🕴 FAMILY TIME ACTIVITIES

- Play "Two Truths and a Lie" as a family. Have every family member come up with two things about themselves that are true and one thing that is a lie. Each member takes a turn telling his three "facts." Everyone must vote on which fact they think is a lie.

- Check out some picture books of the nativity story at the library. Read through them, and look at the pictures. Try to pick out what aspects are in the Bible and what are not in the Bible. *The Animal's Christmas* by Elena Pasquali is a good one.

- Sing "We Three Kings." Talk about how even though we know they weren't kings, it doesn't change the meaning of the song.

DECEMBER 23 Did Jesus Have a Sin Nature?

 A CLOSER LOOK

The question "Did Jesus have a sin nature?" is an interesting one to consider. If He didn't, that would make Him the only perfect human ever born. If He did, then He would have been no different than you and me in our spiritual condition before God. We are celebrating the birth of Jesus in a couple of days, so this is an important theological concept to grasp because of its consequences. Before being able to discuss if Jesus had a sin nature, it is important to understand what a sin nature is and where it came from.

Sin is probably one of the most-used theological words in existence. The Bible helps to define what sin is. First John 3:4 tells us that all sin is lawlessness; sin is breaking the laws of God. Deuteronomy 9:7 tells us that disobedience against God is nothing short of rebellion. Isaiah 59:2 tells us that all sins are an offense to God and separate us from Him completely. Sin came into the human race when Adam and Eve chose to break the commandments of God and ate from the tree of knowledge of good and evil. They rebelled against God by breaking His commandments (Genesis 3:1-15). This is called the original sin by theologians. This is where sin originated for the human race.

Even though we in the 21st century were not alive at the time of the garden incident, we are just as guilty before God. Adam acted as the representative for the whole human race (this is called federal headship). The phrase "in Adam" (1 Corinthians 5:22) is used to describe all humans. We are represented by Adam because the entire human race descends from him (genetically). Just as we inherit our genetics from him, we also inherit a nature that is sinful. We are worthy of God's judgment because of this (Roman 5:12, 18). Adam and Eve's first two sons were Cain and Abel. Evidence of that sin nature being passed down can be seen when Cain murdered Abel (Genesis 4:8). It didn't take long to go from perfection to murder. We, at our core, are beyond wicked (Jeremiah 17:9). Apart from God's grace, a very bleak picture is painted of humanity.

God, through the second part of the Trinity, was brought into this world in the incarnation. Jesus came here with a specific mission: to suffer and die for humanity. He was born as a human, and all humans are born with a sin nature. If Jesus had a sin nature, this would have affected His mission with grave consequences for all of us. Did Jesus have a sin nature? We know that Christ was tempted (Matthew 4), and He didn't give into the temptation from Satan. Being tempted is not a sign of a sin nature, though. Adam and Eve, when they were tempted in the Garden of Eden, did not have a sin nature yet because they were created perfect. We can see from Jesus' life that is recorded in the Gospels that He did not sin while living on earth. In fact, we were told that no sin was ever found in Him. Hebrews 4:15 and 1 John 3:5 makes this point clear with such phrases as "yet He did not sin" and "in Him is no sin."

Furthermore, since a sin nature is passed down from parents to children, the birth of Christ helps to answer this question. Christ's conception was not a normal conception, but rather a miracle of the Holy Spirit (Luke 1:35). Jesus did not have an earthly biological father.

He was Son of God and Son of Man. Jesus was born of a virgin in fulfillment of prophecy (Genesis 3:15; Isaiah 7:14). Some believe that the sin nature is passed down from father to children and this is how Jesus avoided having a sin nature in His human nature. Scripture is silent on this. We do know that Jesus was fully human, but He was also fully God (Colossians 2:9-10). Theologians call this the Hypostatic Union [74]. God is not able to sin; it goes against His nature [75]. The divine part of Jesus's nature precludes Him from having a sin nature. Christ does not have a sin nature; He is the most unique and important child ever born!

Read	Hebrews 4:15
	1 John 3:5

DAILY DEVOTION

If you have spent any amount of time with a three year old, you will know that kids are naughty. They don't have to be taught how to misbehave. (I certainly didn't teach my three year old how to climb the furniture and shove his little brother.) It is something they are born knowing how to do. In fact, they have to be taught how to be good.

This is true for everyone in the whole world, except for one person: Jesus. Jesus was born perfect and never sinned. Can you imagine being perfect? I would love it if I never had to send my son to time out ever again. But I will, because my son has a sin nature, and so do you.

Did you know that before Jesus came, people had to offer sacrifices for their sins? They had to find an animal to offer that did not have any blemishes on it; it had to be perfect. Because Jesus was perfect, He was able to use His body as the ultimate sacrifice for our sins when He died on the cross. After His death, people no longer had to offer animals as sacrifices for their sins because Jesus' death covered it all.

I am so grateful that Jesus died for my sins long before I was even alive. He didn't have to die on the cross, but He did because He loves us so much. Thank You, Jesus!

LET'S TALK

What does it mean to be perfect?

What does it mean to sin?

What are sins that you struggle with?

Why was it important that Jesus was perfect?

★ PRAYER ★

Lord, thank You for sending Jesus to live a perfect life and become the ultimate sacrifice for our sins. Thank You for loving us so passionately. Help us to make good choices and to serve You in all we do.

🧍 FAMILY TIME ACTIVITIES

- Imagine what it would be like to grow up with Jesus as your brother.

- Get a large piece of paper and some markers. Have everyone draw large circles. See who can draw the most perfect large circle. Everyone can try several times. Afterwards, talk about how we can try really hard to be perfect, but only Jesus is truly perfect.

- Read *If Jesus Lived Inside My Heart* by Jill Roman Lord.

- Sing "Joyful, Joyful We Exalt Thee".

$\begin{smallmatrix}\text{DECEMBER}\end{smallmatrix}$24 Why Was This Birth so Important?

 **A CLOSER LOOK**

Over two thousand years ago in a small rural village, a Child was born. Eight days later, His mother and father named Him Jesus as the angel had commanded. We've been digging through the details of His birth for the past twenty-three days. This was clearly a supernatural event in so many ways. But people still ask: What was so important about His birth?

The answer is found in the mission this Child came to accomplish. He was born for a specific purpose. His given name was Jesus. Have you ever stopped to think about what that name means? In the Bible, names are not just given because they sound cool and are the latest trend in Hollywood; they were given because they had meaning attached to them. God had chosen a name with a specific meaning. Jesus comes from the same Hebrew word as Joshua with a meaning of "Jehovah (Yahweh) will save.[76]" An angel told Joseph that Jesus was coming because He would save His people from their sin (Matthew 1:21). Jesus was coming with a specific purpose- the redemption of humanity.

Up until the time of Christ, God had mandated an offering to atone for the sins of the nation of Israel. A sin offering was required (there were several different offerings prescribed in the Old Testament such as sin offerings and peace offerings[77]) to cover sin (Leviticus 4:1-4). An animal had to be killed and its blood spilled as means of sacrificial atonement (atonement can be thought of as a way to pay for sin) for the person who was offering the sin offering. There was a problem with these offerings; they didn't actually cover the sins of the people who offered them. Hebrews 10:4 tells us that *"It is impossible for the blood of bulls and goats to take away sins."* God called His people to offer the sacrifices not because they would cover people's sins, but because it taught the lesson that sin needed to have a sacrifice to cover it.

In yesterday's 'A Closer Look' section , we established that all people (Romans 3:23) are wicked and evil at their core (Jeremiah 17:9). Because of this, a rift exists between them and God. God is a holy God. His holiness demands a payment be made for sin. The price to pay for sin is our death, according to Romans 6:23. There is not a way to pay this price in any other way on our own. This is where Jesus came in. A redeemer had been promised. This redeemer would come along and make an end to the rift sin causes between God and man. Jesus came to fulfill this role in His first advent.

In the Levitical sin offerings, a perfect sacrifice was required. It could have no blemishes (Leviticus 4:3). Jesus was this perfect sacrifice for us (1 Peter 1:19). His life was one that was perfect; no sin was found in Him, from the moment of His birth to the moment He died on the cross. He became our representative on the cross, taking on our sins to pay for them (2 Corinthians 5:21) with His life. Just as Adam acted as our representative in the Garden and passed down a sin nature to all of humanity (Romans 5:12), Christ was our representative on the cross. His death paid the price for sin and *His righteous act resulted in justification and life for all people* (Romans 5:18) who choose to follow Him. Jesus' birth is significant because it launched Him into the ministry that would reconcile humanity to God the Father!

Read   Matthew 1:21

 **DAILY DEVOTION**

It was Sunday morning, and Brandon did not want to go to church. It all seemed pretty silly to him. He couldn't understand how anyone could believe the story about Mary and Joseph and baby Jesus. Why would God send His Son, Jesus, to earth in the first place? It all seemed a little far-fetched.

Brandon's parents had been praying for Brandon for a while now. They knew he did not like going to church and that he did not believe in God. They prayed that God would reveal Himself to Brandon and that Brandon would learn to love and trust Him.

That morning at the breakfast table, Brandon's eyes wandered out the window. There was a huge storm raging around outside. The sky was dark with thunderheads and torrents of rain were pounding against the landscape. The wind was whipping the branches of the big oak tree around like they were paper. And that's when he saw it. A cold, wet figure curled up in a tight ball against the tree. Brandon moved closer to the window and pressed his face against it. He squinted his eyes, trying to see through the rain. Sure enough, it was a baby fox.

The fox looked hungry and was shivering in the rain. He had his nose tucked under a paw, but every moment or two would readjust his body to try and keep out of the rain. Brandon's heart broke at the site of this poor helpless animal out in the cold.

"Brandon, what are you doing? Not in your church clothes!" his mother called after him. But it was too late. Brandon had already grabbed a couple slices of bacon and was out the door. The rain pummeled him as he made his way towards the big oak tree. The fox looked up at Brandon and stiffened his body. Brandon was still several yards away, but he held out the bacon and called through the rain, "It's okay. I won't hurt you. I brought you some food!" As Brandon took another step closer, the fox got up and limped away as quickly as possible.

Brandon was crushed. He trudged back inside and stood at the door, sopping wet. "What is wrong, son?" his father asked with a mouth full of food. "There was a baby fox out there who was lost. He was hungry and shivering in the cold, and he had a hurt paw. I wanted to help him, but he ran away." Brandon's bottom lip began to quiver. He was sure that fox didn't have a chance out there in the storm. "I tried to tell him I wanted to help him, but he couldn't understand me." Brandon wished he could become a fox, just for a moment, so he could explain to the baby fox that he was here to help in a language that that the baby fox would understand. Then his mind drifted to Jesus, and it all made sense. God sent His Son Jesus to earth to speak to us in a language we understand and to save all of humanity.

That morning Brandon gave his heart to Jesus, and his parents praised God that their prayers were answered through a hungry, baby fox.

🧍 LET'S TALK

Why did Brandon not want to go to church?

Why did he wish he could become a fox?

How did that help him understand why God sent Jesus?

⭐ PRAYER ⭐

Lord, thank You for listening to the prayers of Your people.
Thank you for sending Jesus as our Savior.

🧍 FAMILY TIME ACTIVITIES

- Get in the car and go for a drive in the neighborhood, looking at all the colorful lights. Talk about how Jesus is like a light in the dark world.

- Curl up on the couch together with some yummy snacks and watch *The Nativity Story.*

- Read *Jesus Must Be Really Special* by Jennie Bishop.

- Sing "Joy to the World."

DECEMBER 25 — Who Is Jesus to You?

 **A CLOSER LOOK**

Peter and the other disciples had been working with Jesus for over two years, learning from Him, witnessing miracles, and seeing the crowds that followed Him. As they were walking along one day, Jesus asked a simple question to the group, *"Who do men say that I am?"* (Matthew 16:13). The disciples had been around enough to talk to people and get their impressions of whom they thought Jesus was. Peter piped in and said that some thought He was John the Baptist. Peter continued and said that others thought He was Elijah or Jeremiah or some other prophet. (Both Elijah and Jeremiah were powerful speakers who boldly declared the messages that God had given to them. There are prophecies that Elijah would come again [Malachi 4:5], so some people were thinking that Jesus was the fulfillment of these prophecies.) After reviewing the confusion people had over Jesus' identity, Peter boldly declares that He is *"the Christ, the Son of the Living God"* (Matthew 16:16). Peter understood that Jesus was not merely man, but that He was God incarnate, the promised Messiah [78].

Who is Jesus to you? This question has a profound and life altering meaning. Is He just some good teacher from Nazareth who riled up the religious establishment and was put to death by the Romans? Or is He the Son of God? Today we celebrate the greatest gift that has been ever offered to humanity, the gift of salvation. Ephesians 2:8-9 says, "For it is by grace you have been saved, through faith—and this is not from yourselves, it is the gift of God— not by works, so that no one can boast." God's gift to us is Christ and the work that He accomplished on the cross. We gain access to this gift by putting our faith in Christ, not by anything we do on our own. Romans 10:9-10 tells us exactly how to put our faith in Christ. Paul writes and says, "If you declare with your mouth, 'Jesus is Lord,' and believe in your heart that God raised him from the dead, you will be saved. For it is with your heart that you believe and are justified, and it is with your mouth that you profess your faith and are saved."

Putting your faith in Christ is as simple as the ABC's.

A – Admit that you're a sinner. This is recognizing the fact that we can't redeem ourselves

> before the law of God. We need someone to do it for us.

B – Believe in Christ's sacrifice. Believe that Jesus died on the cross and paid the price

> for your sins. Believe that He didn't stay dead, but He rose again three days later. Believe that He conquered death and is now sitting in Heaven at the right hand of God the Father.

C- Choose to live for Him. This is choosing daily to surrender our lives to Him and follow His leading as our Lord.

In John 14:6, Jesus boldly declares that He "is the way, the truth and the life. No one comes to the Father except through Him."

Will you come to Jesus? He's waiting for you![79]

Read	Matthew 16:15

 **DAILY DEVOTION**

Merry Christmas! We have spent the last twenty-four days learning about the miraculous story of Jesus' birth. We learned about Mary finding out from the angel Gabriel that she was pregnant. We learned about her visit to Elizabeth, who was pregnant with John the Baptist. We learned about Elizabeth's husband, Zacharias, who was struck mute until John was born. We learned about the census and Mary and Joseph's journey to Nazareth. We learned about the star and the shepherds and the wise men and the three gifts. But most importantly, we learned about the birth of a perfect Baby Boy who was both human and God. This Baby Boy grew up to be a man who loved all of humanity so much, He gave His life on the cross as a perfect sacrifice. He did this for you! Then three days later, He arose from the dead, overcoming death, and giving us all the chance to spend eternity with Him.

Tomorrow will be December 26, and our Christmas celebration will be over. So what do we do now? I think the famous spiritual "Go Tell it on the Mountain" says it best:

Go tell it on the mountain

Over the hills and everywhere,

Go tell it on the mountain,

Our Jesus Christ is born.

LET'S TALK

What is your favorite part of the nativity story?

Do you believe that Jesus is the Son of God?

How can we tell our friends about Jesus?

★ PRAYER ★

Lord, we praise You because You planned from the beginning of time to give us a Savior. Help us to tell everyone we know about the good news of Jesus!

FAMILY TIME ACTIVITIES

- Talk about salvation. If your kids believe that Jesus is Lord and that God raised Him from the dead (Romans 10:9), then they may be ready to accept Jesus as their Lord and Savior. (See Appendix D for a salvation prayer you could lead them through if they are ready.)

- Celebrate! Enjoy dessert, play games, spend time with loved ones.

- Read *I've Got a Job To Do* by Dandi Daley Mackall.

- Sing "Go Tell it on the Mountain."

- Give Jesus a gift by serving the needy. Let your children choose an item from one of the many catalogs that provide food, animals, clothing, clean water, etc. for people living in poverty across the world. Make it a Christmas tradition.

Check out one of these great ministries:

https://www.compassion.ca/shop/

http://www.samaritanspurse.org/our-ministry/gift-catalog/

http://harvestofhope.org

http://donate.worldvision.org

http://www.gfa.org/gift/

Biography

Scott and Sarah Nichols are passionate about serving God and helping others live intentionally for Him. They have been married for six years and have two young boys who keep them laughing. They are humbled by God's grace and mercy in their lives.

Scott has his bachelor's degree in political science from Portland State University and a Master of Divinity degree from Multnomah University. He is a youth pastor by day and an aviation geek by night. Scott hopes to someday pursue a Doctorate of Ministry.

Sarah has her bachelor's degree in special education and her Master of Education degree in teaching reading through Grand Canyon University. She is the author at www.simplelifeabundantlife.com where she encourages people to live the abundant life God has for them through faith, family, food, and healthy living.

White Dove Photography

Together Scott and Sarah are excited to share their hearts with you through this Christmas devotional. They pray it will bless your family immensely. Feel free to contact them at Scott@ simplelifeabundantlife.com or Sarah@simplelifeabundantlife.com.

Appendix A Prophecy Memory Cards

A PDF version of this printable is available at http://morethanaholidaydevo.com/printables/.

"Joseph also went up from Galilee, from the city of Nazareth, to Judea, to the city of David which is called Bethlehem, because he was of the house and family of David...while they were there the days were completed for her to give birth." Luke 2:4,6	"So Joseph got up and took the Child and his mother while it was still night, and left for Egypt." Matthew 2:14
"But as for you Bethlehem... From you One will go forth for me to be ruler in Israel. His goings forth are from long ago, from the days of eternity." Micah 5:2	"When Israel was a youth I loved him, and out of Egypt I called my Son." Hosea 11:1

"Thus says the Lord, "A voice is heard in Ramah, lamentation and bitter weeping. Rachel is weeping for her children; She refuses to be comforted for her children, because they are no more." Jeremiah 31:15	"Then when Herod saw that he had been tricked by the magi, he became very enraged, and sent and slew all the male children...from two years old and under..." Matthew 2:16
"But God will redeem me from the realm of the dead; he will surely take me to himself." Psalm 49:15	"The angel said to the women, "Do not be afraid, for I know that you are looking for Jesus, who was crucified. He is not here; he has risen, just as he said. Come and see the place where he lay." Matthew 28:5-6

"After the Lord Jesus had spoken to them, he was taken up into heaven and he sat at the right hand of God." Matthew 16:19	"The Lord says to my lord: "Sit at my right hand until I make your enemies a footstool for your feet.""" Psalm 110:1

Appendix B

A PDF version of this printable is available at
<u>morethanaholidaydevo.com</u>

Appendix C

A PDF version of this printable is available at
morethanaholidaydevo.com

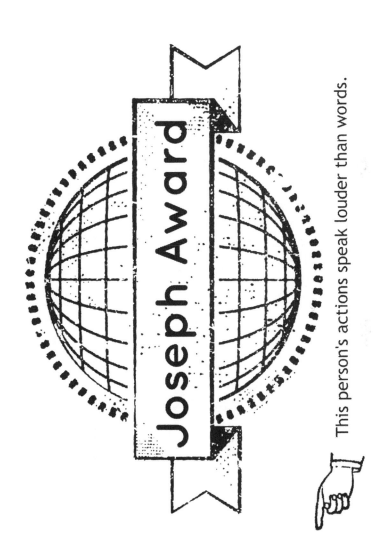

Appendix D

Salvation Prayer

Dear Lord,

I know that I am a sinner. I confess those sins to You and ask You to forgive me. I believe that You are God and that You sent Jesus to earth as a baby. I believe He lived a perfect life and died on the cross as a sacrifice for my sins. I believe that three days later He rose again, conquering death. I believe He is the way, the truth, and the life. Please come live inside of me. Help me to make good decisions and to seek You with my whole heart. I love You, Lord, and thank You for Your gift of salvation.

In Jesus' Name,

Amen

*If you or someone in your family prayed this prayer for the first time, we would love to hear about it and rejoice with you. Send an email to Scott@simplelifeabundantlife.com.

References

[1] Tacitus, *Annals* 15.44

[2] Pliny, Letters, transl. by William Melmoth, rev. by W.M.L. Hutchinson (Cambridge: Harvard Univ. Press, 1935), vol. II, X:96, cited in Habermas, *The Historical Jesus*, 199.

[3] Flavius Josephus, *Antiquities of the Jews, 18.3.3.* 2013. Early Jewish Writings – Josephus. 7/28/13 <http://www.earlyjewishwritings.com/text/josephus/ant18.html>

[4] Brian. "Extra Biblical Evidence for Jesus."*Know It's True | "...so that you may know the certainty of the things you have been taught." - Luke 1:4.* N.p., n.d. Web. 6 Sept. 2013. <http://knowitstrue.com/extra-biblical-evidence-for-jesus/>.

[5] Strauss, Richard L. "Impossible Things Do Happen." June 28, 2004. Bible. org. 7/23/2013 <https://bible.org/seriespage/impossible-things-do-happen%E2%80%94i-story-zacharias-and-elizabethi>

[6] MacArthur, John. *One perfect life: the complete story of Jesus.* Nashville, Tenn.: Thomas Nelson, 2012. Print.pg 42 see also 1 Chronicles 24:10

[7] <https://bible.org/seriespage/impossible-things-do-happen%E2%80%94i-story-zacharias-and-elizabethi>

[8] Flavius Josephus, *Antiquities of the Jews.* 18.5.2. ,http://www.earlyjewishwritings. com/text/josephus/ant18.html>

[9] Vörös, Győző "Machaerus: Where Salome Danced and John the Baptist Was Beheaded." Biblical Archaeology Review, September/October 2012, 7/28/13 <http://members.bib-arch.org/publication.asp?PubID=BSBA&Volume=38&Issue=5&ArticleID=2>

[10] Stormy Rich, Florida High School Student, Barred From School Bus After Reporting Bullying Of Special Needs Student." *Breaking News and Opinion on The Huffington Post.* N.p., n.d. Web. 6 Sept. 2013. <http://www.huffingtonpost. com/2012/05/28/stormy-rich-florida-high-_n_1551350.html>

[11] Category. "Herod the Great - Ruthless King of the Jews." *Christianity - About Christianity and Living the Christian Life.* N.p., n.d. Web. 6 Sept. 2013. <http://christianity.about.com/od/newtestamentpeople/a/JZ-Herod-The-Great.htm>.

[12] Antipater was made procurator over Judah in 47BC by Pompey. "Herod (king of Judaea) – Encyclopeia Britannica. – *Encyclopedia Britannica.* N.p.,n.d.. Web 6 Sept, 2013.< http://www.britannica.com/EBchecked/topic/263437/Herod>

[13] Montefiore, Simon. *Jerusalem: the biography.* New York: Alfred A. Knopf, 2011. Print.).

[14] Hagner, Donald A., Glenn W. Barker, David A. Hubbard, and Bruce M. Metzger. *Matthew 1-13.* [7. Dr.]. ed. Dallas, Tex.: Word Books, Publ., 2000. Print pg 37

[15] "Researchers Diagnose Herod the Great - ABC News." *ABCNews.com - Breaking News, Latest News & Top Video News - ABC News.* N.p., n.d. Web. 6 Sept. 2013. <http://abcnews.go.com/Technology/story?id=98107&page=1>.

[16] This doctrine is called the perpetual virginity of Mary – for more about this doctrine see :

Mary: Ever Virgin. *"Catholic Answers"* N.p,n.d. Web 6 Sept 2013. <http://www.catholic.com/tracts/mary-ever-virgin>

Apologetics Press - Did Jesus Have Fleshly Half-Brothers?." *Apologetics Press | Bible Contradiction |.* N.p., n.d. Web. 6 Sept. 2013. <http://www.apologeticspress.org/apcontent.aspx?category=11&article=1271>[17]

[17] "Mary the Blessed Virgin - Saints & Angels - Catholic Online." *Catholic Online.* N.p., n.d. Web. 6 Sept. 2013. <http://www.catholic.org/saints/saint.php?saint_id=4967>

[18] For more information on the Davidic Covenant see: "What is the Davidic covenant?." *Bible Questions Answered.* N.p., n.d. Web. 6 Sept. 2013. <http://www.gotquestions.org/Davidic-covenant.html>.

[19] Fairchild, Mary. "Mary The Mother Of Jesus - Profile Of The Virgin Mary."*Christianity - About Christianity and Living the Christian Life.* N.p., n.d. Web. 6 Sept. 2013. <http://christianity.about.com/od/newtestamentpeople/p/mary-motherjesus.htm>

[20] Joseph, James, Judas, and Simon from a list in Mark 6:3 and Matthew 13:55-56

[21] "When were Joseph and Mary considered married?." *Bible Questions Answered.* N.p., n.d. Web. 6 Sept. 2013. <http://www.gotquestions.org/Joseph-and-Mary.html>.

[22] "Where was Joseph when Jesus was an adult?." *Bible Questions Answered.* N.p., n.d. Web. 6 Sept. 2013. <http://www.gotquestions.org/Joseph-Jesus.html>.

[23] Ibid

[24] Daniel 10:13, 10:21, & 12:1, and Jude 9. An archangel is mentioned in 1 Thessalonians 4:16, but is not named Michael.

[25] "7 Biblical Facts about the Angel Gabriel | Logos Talk: The Logos Bible Software Blog." *Logos Talk: The Logos Bible Software Blog | A blog about Logos Bible Software—the software, the company, the people, and more.* N.p., n.d. Web. 6 Sept. 2013. <http://blog.logos.com/2012/12/7-biblical-facts-about-the-angel-gabriel/>

[26] "Historical timeline of Daniel." *Pytlik dot com.* N.p., n.d. Web. 6 Sept. 2013. <http://www.pytlik.com/observe/daniel/timeline.html>

[27] "The Roman Empire: in the First Century. The Roman Empire. Emperors. Augustus | PBS." *PBS: Public Broadcasting Service.* N.p., n.d. Web. 6 Sept. 2013. <http://

www.pbs.org/empires/romans/empire/augustus.html>

Gill, N.S.. "Tiberius - Roman Emperor."*Ancient / Classical History - Ancient Greece & Rome & Classics Research Guide.* N.p., n.d. Web. 6 Sept. 2013. <http://ancienthistory.about.com/od/tiberius.htm>

[28] "What Year Did Jesus Die?." *Patheos | Hosting the Conversation on Faith.* N.p., n.d. Web. 6 Sept. 2013. <http://www.patheos.com/blogs/jesuscreed/2012/06/03/what-year-did-jesus-die/>.

[29] Akin, Jimmy. "7 clues tell us *precisely* when Jesus died (the year, month, day, and hour revealed) |Blogs | NCRegister.com." *National Catholic Register | NCRegister.com.* N.p., n.d. Web. 6 Sept. 2013. <http://www.ncregister.com/blog/jimmy-akin/when-precisely-did-jesus-die-the-year-month-day-and-hour-revealed>.

[30] "Mary's Magnificat | Grace Valley Christian Center." *Grace Valley Christian Center.* N.p., n.d. Web. 6 Sept. 2013. <http://www.gracevalley.org/sermon_tran/2000/marys_magnficat.html#.UfyCN12sjPo>

[31] "Meditation on the Magnificat Sunday Evening Message - Desiring God." *Home - Desiring God.* N.p., n.d. Web. 6 Sept. 2013. <http://www.desiringgod.org/resource-library/sermons/meditation-on-the-magnificat>.

[32] For more information on the intertestimental period see the website Stedman, Ray C. "The 400 Years Between the Old and New Testaments." *Templemount.org* <http://www.templemount.org/0240.html>

[33] Oard, Mike, and John Reed. "Quirinius census luke." *creation.com.* N.p., n.d. Web. 6 Sept. 2013. <http://creation.com/quirinius-census-luke>

[34] Flavius Josephus, *Antiquities of the Jews, 18.1.* 2013. Early Jewish Writings – Josephus. 7/28/13 <http://www.earlyjewishwritings.com/text/josephus/ant18.html> This is the only census recorded outside the Bible near to this point in time.

[35] Josephus, *Antiquities* XVII.355 & XVIII.1–2

[36] When did the Luke 2 census occur? • ChristianAnswers.Net." *Christian Answers Network [Home] • Multilingual answers, reviews, ministry resources, and more! • ChristianAnswers.Net.* N.p., n.d. Web. 10 Sept. 2013. <http://christiananswers.net/q-aiia/census-luke2.html>

"A Brief Comment on the Census in Luke 2." *Associates for Biblical Research.* N.p., n.d. Web. 10 Sept. 2013. <http://www.biblearchaeology.org/post/2008/10/16/A-Brief-Comment-on-the-Census-in-Luke-2.aspx>

[37] When did the Luke 2 census occur? • ChristianAnswers.Net." *Christian Answers Network [Home] • Multilingual answers, reviews, ministry resources, and more! • ChristianAnswers.Net.* N.p., n.d. Web. 10 Sept. 2013. <http://christiananswers.net/q-aiia/census-luke2.html>

[38] Oard, Mike, and John Reed. "Quirinius census luke." *creation.com.* N.p., n.d. Web. 10 Sept. 2013. <http://creation.com/quirinius-census-luke>

[39] Hoenher, Harold., *Chronological Aspects of the Life of Christ*, p. 21, Zondervan, 1978

[40] "A Brief Comment on the Census in Luke 2." *Associates for Biblical Research*. N.p., n.d. Web. 10 Sept. 2013. <http://www.biblearchaeology.org/post/2008/10/16/A-Brief-Comment-on-the-Census-in-Luke-2.aspx>

[41] "A Brief Comment on the Census in Luke 2." *Associates for Biblical Research*. N.p., n.d. Web. 10 Sept. 2013. <http://www.biblearchaeology.org/post/2008/10/16/A-Brief-Comment-on-the-Census-in-Luke-2.aspx>

This record states *"I register Pakebkis, the son born to me and wife, Taasies and Tapis in the 10th year of the reign of Tiberius Claudius Caesar Augustus Germanicus Imperator, and request that the name of my aforesaid son Pakebis is to be entered on the list."*

[42] Oard, Mike, and John Reed. "Quirinius census luke." *creation.com*. N.p., n.d. Web. 10 Sept. 2013. <http://creation.com/quirinius-census-luke>

[43] "No Room for an Inn - Answers in Genesis." *Answers in Genesis - Creation, Evolution, Christian Apologetics* . N.p., n.d. Web. 10 Sept. 2013. <http://www.answersingenesis.org/get-answers/features/christmas-no-room-for-inn>[44] "No Room in the What? | Christianity Today." *Christianity Today | Theology, Church, Culture*. N.p., n.d. Web. 10 Sept. 2013. <http://www.christianitytoday.com/ct/2007/december-web-only/151-33.0.html>.

[45] Ibid

[46] Ibid

[47] " Phatne - New Testament Greek Lexicon - New American Standard." *Bible Study Tools Online – Verses, Commentaries, Concordances, Verses, Parallel Versions*. N.p., n.d. Web. 10 Sept. 2013. <http://www.biblestudytools.com/lexicons/

[48] "The Manger and the Inn." *Associates for Biblical Research*. N.p., n.d. Web. 10 Sept. 2013. <http://www.biblearchaeology.org/post/2008/11/08/The-Manger-and-the-Inn.aspx>

[49] "Was Jesus Born in a House? - Answers in Genesis." *Answers in Genesis - Creation, Evolution, Christian Apologetics* . N.p., n.d. Web. 10 Sept. 2013. <http://www.answersingenesis.org/articles/2009/12/22/was-jesus-born-in-a-house>.

[50] Ibid

[51] MacArthur one perfect life pg 56

[52] "What is the Shekinah glory?." *Bible Questions Answered*. N.p., n.d. Web. 10 Sept. 2013. <http://www.gotquestions.org/shekinah-glory.html>

[53] "Shekinah | Define Shekinah at Dictionary.com." *Dictionary.com - Free Online English Dictionary*. N.p., n.d. Web. 10 Sept. 2013. <http://dictionary.reference.com/browse/shekinah>

[54] "Strong's Greek: 32. , (aggelos) -- an angel, messenger." *Bible Suite: Online Bible, Concordance, Topical, Strong's, Greek and Hebrew.* N.p., n.d. Web. 10 Sept. 2013. <http://biblesuite.com/greek/32.htm>

[55] Strong's Greek: 4990. -- a savior, deliverer." *Bible Suite: Online Bible, Concordance, Topical, Strong's, Greek and Hebrew.* N.p., n.d. Web. 10 Sept. 2013. <http://biblesuite.com/greek/4990.htm>

[56] Ibid

[57] "Strong's Greek: 5547. (Christos) -- the Anointed One, Messiah, Christ." *Bible Suite: Online Bible, Concordance, Topical, Strong's, Greek and Hebrew.* N.p., n.d. Web. 10 Sept. 2013. <http://biblesuite.com/greek/5547.htm

[58] "Strong's Greek: 5547. (Christos) -- the Anointed One, Messiah, Christ." *Bible Suite: Online Bible, Concordance, Topical, Strong's, Greek and Hebrew.* N.p., n.d. Web. 10 Sept. 2013. <http://biblesuite.com/greek/5547.htm

MacArthur *One Perfect Life* pg 56

[59] Lord, the. "Strong's Greek: 2962. (kurios) -- lord, master." *Bible Suite: Online Bible, Concordance, Topical, Strong's, Greek and Hebrew.* N.p., n.d. Web. 10 Sept. 2013. <http://biblesuite.com/greek/2962.htm>

[60] Lord, the. "Strong's Greek: 2962. (kurios) -- lord, master." *Bible Suite: Online Bible, Concordance, Topical, Strong's, Greek and Hebrew.* N.p., n.d. Web. 10 Sept. 2013. <http://biblesuite.com/greek/2962.htm>

MacArthur *One Perfect Life* pg 56

[61] "Strong's Greek: 1515. - one, peace, quietness, rest. ." *Bible Suite: Online Bible, Concordance, Topical, Strong's, Greek and Hebrew.* N.p., n.d. Web. 10 Sept. 2013. <http://biblesuite.com/greek/1515.htm>

[62] magi, the. "Strong's Greek: 3097. (magos) -- a Magian, i.e. an (Oriental) astrologer, by impl. a magician." *Bible Suite: Online Bible, Concordance, Topical, Strong's, Greek and Hebrew.* N.p., n.d. Web. 10 Sept. 2013. <http://biblesuite.com/greek/3097.htm>

[63] "The Star of Bethlehem." *Associates for Biblical Research.* N.p., n.d. Web. 10 Sept. 2013. <http://www.biblearchaeology.org/post/2005/10/17/The-Star-of-Bethlehem.aspx>.

[64] Ibid

[65] For a much more detailed discussion on the conjunction see - "The Star of Bethlehem: the facts about the star of Christ." *The Star of Bethlehem: the facts about the star of Christ.* N.p., n.d. Web. 10 Sept. 2013. <http://www.bethlehemstar.net>

[66] "Why Did the Magi Bring Gold, Frankincense and Myrrh? – Biblical Archaeol-

ogy Society." *Bringing the Ancient World to Life - Biblical Archaeology Society.* N.p., n.d. Web. 10 Sept. 2013. <http://www.biblicalarchaeology.org/daily/people-cultures-in-the-bible/jesus-historical-jesus/why-did-the-magi-bring-gold-frankincense-and-myrrh/>

[67] MarArthur *One Perfect Life* pg 62

[68] Leston, Stephen, and Christopher D. Hudson. *The Bible in world history: how history and scripture intersect.* Uhrichsville, Ohio: Barbour Pub., 2011. Print. Pg228

[69] Ibid

[70] Ibid

[71] Leston, Stephen, and Christopher D. Hudson. *The Bible in world history: how history and scripture intersect.* Uhrichsville, Ohio: Barbour Pub., 2011. Print. Pg228-229

[72] Luke 2 - IVP New Testament Commentaries." *Bible Gateway Commentaries.* N.p., n.d. Web. 9 Sept. 2013. < http://www.biblegateway.com/resources/commentaries/IVP-NT/Luke/Witness-Man-Woman-Temple>

[73] MacArthur *One Perfect Life* pg59

[74] "What is the hypostatic union? | Christian Apologetics and Research Ministry."-*CARM - Christian Apologetics and Research Ministry.* N.p., n.d. Web. 10 Sept. 2013. <http://carm.org/hypostatic-union>.

[75] For a fuller discussion on this topic see http://carm.org/questions/about-god/can-god-do-everything-including-sin

[76] MacArthur, John . "The Significance of the Virgin Birth." *Grace To You.* N.p., n.d. Web. 10 Sept. 2013. <http://www.gty.org/blog/B111221>

[77] See this website for more details about the various kinds of offerings required in the Old Testament –

priests, the. "The 5 Levitical Offerings (Bible History Online)." *Bible History Online Images and Resources for Biblical History.* N.p., n.d. Web. 10 Sept. 2013. <http://www.bible-history.com/tabernacle/TAB4The_5_Levitical_Offerings.htm

[78] This passage is found in Matthew 16:13-20, Mark 8:27-30 and Luke 9:18-21[79] II Peter 3:9 The Lord is not slow in keeping his promise, as some understand slowness. Instead he is patient with you, not wanting anyone to perish, but everyone to come to repentance.

Made in the USA
Lexington, KY
07 December 2016